## Praise for Claire S
## From Wallflower to Sunflower

Claire Schrader's new confidence-building system, the Sunflower Effect fills in the gaps where assertiveness training and other techniques leave off. If you are a wallflower and you've tried practically everything else, read this book and discover that all the things that people have been saying about you are plainly not true.

**Raymond Aaron, NY Times Best Selling Author**

Claire Schrader's new book gives hope to anyone who finds themselves trapped as a wallflower. I have seen for myself how easily and quickly Claire can help people step out of their mental 'prison', which they may have been stuck in for years and instead in a playful manner reconnect with their natural inner confidence, joy and freedom. I find that Claire's methods and compassionate approach compliments hypnotherapy as clients can actually practise, explore and build on what they achieve through hypnotherapy, whilst being held in a safe space. You don't need to be a wallflower anymore; you can become the sunflower that you really are. This book will show you how.

**Kirsten Dahlerup, Clinical Hypnotherapist and NLP Master practitioner**

*From Wallflower to Sunflower* is an essential companion for anyone just setting out across this daunting landscape, to help build the necessary bridges and create the foundation for reaching an individually defined, positive personal destination. It includes a highly detailed account of the author's self-development journey, its setbacks and challenges - often full of pain and doubt - but ultimately one of self-discovery, transformation and resolution. There are comprehensive exercises, strongly reflecting the type of work done during face-to-face sessions and on group courses at Making Moves. There is access to online resources to back-up and intensify the exercises presented throughout the book. As someone who uses the Bach Flower remedy system I found useful parallels between the extended metaphors of the author's Wallflower and Sunflower states, which define attitudes towards our lives, emotions and imbalances.

**Fran Singer Artist, Teacher and Therapist**

I liked this book a lot. It is clearly and engagingly written, supportive and very accessible. It's almost as if I can hear Claire talking, which is a fantastic skill in a writer. Throughout the book and the numerous examples, we see Claire's ability to create a safe space so that people can take the risks that enable them to start to believe in themselves. Highly recommended.

**Robin Shohet, Centre for Supervision and Team Development, editor of** *Passionate Supervision,* **and** *Supervision as Transformation*

Claire is a marvellously ego-less workshop leader. She empowered a bunch of potential stars to twinkle and shine – I ended up feeling like a 1000-watt light bulb.

**Scilla Ellsworthy, peace builder, TED Talk speaker, and author of** *Pioneering the Possible: awakened leadership for a world that works*

# From Wallflower to Sunflower

## The Quiet Person's Guide to Natural Self-Confidence

Claire Schrader

FROM WALLFLOWER TO SUNFLOWER

the quiet person's guide to natural self confidence

First edition published by 10-10-10 Publishing

122-445 Apple Creek Blvd. Markham, Canada

L3R 9X7

Copyright ©2016 by Claire Schrader London, England, United Kingdom www.makingmoves.net

E: info@makingmoves.net | P: +44 (0) 20 8144 2374

All Rights Reserved

No part of this book may be reproduced in any form, by photocopying or by electronic or mechanical means, including information storage or retrieval systems, without permission in writing from both the copyright owner and the publisher of this book. This book is not intended to give any legal, medical, and/or psychological advice to the readers.

ISBN-13: 978-1539113096

ISBN-10: 1539113094

Printed in the United States of America

# Contents

Praise for *From Wallflower to Sunflower* .................. i
Dedication .................................................................. vii
Acknowledgments ....................................................... ix
About the Author ........................................................ xi
Foreword .................................................................... xiii

Chapter 1: No One Wants to be a Wallflower .............. 1
*Why more and more people are identifying themselves as wallflowers*

Chapter 2: The Secret of the Stars ............................. 13
*The secret that ex-wallflower movie stars know about (and most people don't) that enabled them to fulfil their dreams*

Chapter 3: The Making of the Wallflower .................. 23
*The biggest mistake that wallflowers make when they're trying to build confidence*

Chapter 4: The End of the Wallflower ........................ 35
*How I put an end to my wallflower existence and changed my prospects in a matter of a few short months*

Chapter 5: The Perks of Being a Wallflower ............... 51
*The unique qualities of wallflowers that are often overlooked and how to change how you see yourself*

Chapter 6: The Sunflower Effect .......................................................... 73

*The Missing Link that will move you from wallflower to sunflower - even if you have zero self-belief and low expectations of what you can achieve*

Chapter 7: The Fastest Way of Becoming a Sunflower ...................... 91

*Your magic power to break old habits and create new patterns of confident behaviour that's been with you from the beginning - but you didn't know it*

Chapter 8: Your Secret Weapon to Building Lasting Confidence ..... 109

*Why it can be so hard to build lasting self-confidence - and how to overcome your toughest obstacles*

Chapter 9: It's Your Turn to Shine ..................................................... 129

*Moving out of the shadows to the place where the sunflowers (the confident people) live*

Chapter 10: Living Your Life as a Sunflower ..................................... 137

*Tools and resources that will support you continuing on the path to becoming the person you've always dreamed of being*

Courses to Support You ..................................................................... 167

# Dedication

For Sue Jennings, without whom this book and the Sunflower Effect would never have seen the light of day. Sue's pioneering work, anthropological research and theoretical understanding, is the underpinning of many of the ideas and concepts expressed in this book. I am indebted to her discoveries over 50 years and the remarkable process she has developed, in parallel with many others, which has brought such deep transformation to people who had given up hope that they would ever change.

# Acknowledgments

This book is a result of a lifetime of experiences and there are many people who encouraged me on my path. First, I would like to acknowledge all the experiences and conditions that made me into a wallflower. Without them, this book and the Sunflower Effect would never have come about.

I would also like to thank the unknown doctor who started me thinking that I could do more than I thought I could, and the unknown nurse who set me off on this remarkable life-changing path. I would like to acknowledge the many teachers and organisations who believed in me, inspired me or opened up possibilities in me: Philip Roberts, Andy Harmon, John Muirhead, the Actors Institute, Insight Seminars, Sue Jennings, Steve Mitchell, Anna Chesner, Danusia Malina-Derben, Yollana Shore, Raymond Aaron and countless others who have inspired me and influenced my thinking that are too numerous to mention here.

I would like to thank my partner, Dick, who has supported me throughout the extremely long and slow process of writing this book, as I remained buried in my computer when the sun was shining brightly. My thanks for his detailed and insightful edits and feedback that has made this a much better book than I could have written.

Finally, my gratitude to the thousand-or-so men and women who have participated in my courses and workshops over the last two decades, and whose moving stories, courage and trust in this remarkable process, have contributed to my understanding of what it takes for a wallflower to achieve their fullest and deepest potential. Please note that to protect their confidentiality, the names have been changed of those whose stories are included in this book.

## About Claire

Claire Schrader started out in life as the proverbial wallflower – until she found a way to break out of her shell and acquire some of the skills that the most successful people naturally have. This, she discovered years later, was the same way that countless ex-wallflower movie stars, musicians, comedians, politicians and entrepreneurs had set themselves free from similar handicaps.

As a result, she has achieved things that wouldn't have been possible if she hadn't escaped her wallflower identity. This included pursuing a career in the theatre: performing in young people's theatre, fringe and small-scale touring. For many years too, she played the alternative comedy circuit with her fire-eating act, "La Dame de Flamme", which included a royal function in the vicinity of the Queen. Her first play, *Corryvreckan* (produced at the Old Red Lion Theatre, London 1990), was short listed for Best Play at the 1991 Charrington Fringe Theatre Awards and won an Arts Council Award. For many years she taught in drama schools, she's given presentations at conferences, and run powerful programmes in business for advertising professionals, C.E.O.'s and Organisational Development Consultants. She later trained as a dramatherapist, and for six years was coordinator of the performance programme at The Studio Upstairs. In 1997, she set up Making Moves and over many years developed the Sunflower Effect. She has been leading the way in the field of confidence building through her innovative methods, challenging many widely held beliefs and changing the lives of countless individuals for whom other methods had failed to achieve the desired result. She has offered her courses and workshops in Portugal, the Netherlands, San Francisco and Greece (Skyros Holidays).

Claire has appeared on The Chrissy B Show and Love Talk, for Sky TV. She has also been featured on Radio 4, and in numerous magazines: *She, Marie Claire* (Malaysia), *Positive Health, Kindred Spirit,* and *Woman's World.*

She edited Ritual Theatre: *the power of dramatic ritual in personal development groups and clinical practice* (Jessica Kingsley 2012) and her chapter "Breaking through the Walls of Shyness" was published in *the Routledge International Handbook of Dramatherapy* (Routledge 2016). Her website www.makingmoves.net provides an extensive resource of articles and information on confidence, shyness, social anxiety, and public speaking.

# Foreword

You need top-notch communication skills if you want to get along in today's world. If you're a wallflower and haven't got those skills, you're at a distinct disadvantage. It's not because you are less talented or have poor ideas, in fact, you're probably more talented than most. It's just that you have this knack of remaining invisible. Sadly, many of the existing confidence building methods do too little to improve your prospects.

When I first met Claire Schrader, I found it hard to believe that she was identified as a wallflower. I was struck by how alive and vibrant she was, and how well she was able to communicate under pressure. She too, had a quiet confidence that impressed me. I didn't realize that what I was seeing was the Sunflower Effect in action: the highly effective system that Claire has developed, based on her own experience of transforming her life.

Claire's new book, *From Wallflower to Sunflower,* maps out a surprisingly simple way to access hidden aspects of yourself that's a real game changer in the field of confidence building. It will show how you can move from the sidelines and find the part of yourself that is naturally able to shine. This is what Claire calls your "Sunflower". It's not just another HOW-TO book on confidence, full of techniques and promises that you can never see yourself actually doing.

In fact, there is nothing really new about the Sunflower Effect. Marilyn Monroe, Robin Williams, David Bowie and countless other stars have experienced the same difficulties, but they too hit on the same simple secret that Claire had. Not only that: they stepped out into the limelight and exhibited the exact opposite of wallflower behaviour. You can't really imagine wallflowers behaving in such a flamboyant way, and yet quite clearly it is entirely possible.

Claire has spent nearly twenty years of carefully honing and developing the Sunflower Effect to its present form. If you are a wallflower and you've tried practically everything else, read this book and start to change your prospects.

You will discover that all the things that people have been saying about you are plainly not true.

Raymond Aaron

New York Times Bestselling Author of *Chicken Soup for the Parents' Soul, Chicken Soup for the Canadian Soul, and Double your Income Doing What You Love*

www.aaron.com

# Chapter 1

# No One Wants to be a Wallflower

**Why more and more people are identifying themselves as wallflowers**

Do you wait in the wings; unable to participate in the way you want to, feeling deep down there is another "you" that is longing to come out? Even if you are in the centre of the room, it feels as if you are hugging the edges of the room, shut off from everyone else – invisible, unseen and unnoticed - **and yet glaringly visible.**

"*Everyone can see you being so quiet,*" the voice in your head is continuously telling you. "*They can see just how ridiculous you look. They're wondering why you aren't saying something. They're looking at you expecting you to say something, and you're still not saying anything. But if you say something now they'll think it sounds stupid and that will be even worse, so better to stay quiet so no one notices you.*"

The voice inside you says all this and more, telling you all the reasons why it's better to stay on the sidelines, really believing that it's helping you. There seems to be no way of switching it off. So either you find a way of getting out of the situation, or you do anything to avoid it altogether, or you stay as quiet as possible and slink away, hoping no one has noticed that you didn't say anything.

## You are not alone

You would be surprised how many people feel like this; people you'd never call a wallflower, people who you would assume feel a lot more confident than you do. I've heard this story, almost word for word, over and over again from highly intelligent, sensitive and able people with an enormous amount to offer.

If you are experiencing the painful place of the wallflower in your life right now, let me reassure you. For many years, I felt like this on a daily basis, particularly in any kind of group situation. However, I have completely changed this aspect of my experience – and it wasn't so hard. I actually got over the most debilitating aspects of being a wallflower pretty quickly, as I will be describing in Chapter 4.

This book is for you too, whether there are only some situations and conditions when you experience yourself as a wallflower.

## No one wants to be a wallflower

If you feel like a wallflower, or feel seen as a wallflower by other people, it's very likely that you wish you weren't. Yet it seems you have no other choice than to live like a wallflower, preferring the sidelines over the spotlight, preferring to watch and observe rather than participating - so much of the time you feel separated from the action, cut off from other people, not included, apart. It is this isolation that feels so painful.

This experience may be with you as a day-in-day-out experience or it may appear just in certain situations (you may be pretty confident in most areas but there's one area that sends you to the sidelines). Or maybe you were confident when younger, then much later in life you lost confidence and now you find yourself suddenly back on the sidelines. "How can I get back what I lost?" you ask yourself. It's easier said than done.

You probably already know what you **should do** if you want to stop being a wallflower. You should get out more; be more sociable; just speak up. Behave how the confident people behave; try this technique or that; and stop being so afraid of what other people are thinking of you. The truth of it is - that you'd love to be doing what comes so easily to other people, but you can't. **It's simply impossible.**

### What is holding you back?

What is stopping you from participating in life the way you want to? My clients typically represent this obstacle as a wall that stands between them and other people, which feels impossible to break down. I have battled with it myself, and like you, my attempts to break the wall down were utterly futile. For most wallflowers any attempt to change this situation leads to disappointment and failure, deepening your sense of powerlessness, which in effect increases the power of the wall over you.

What I didn't understand before was that these were **psychological walls,** created by my own defence system to **protect me.** This is the same defence system that created that powerful voice in your head that can't be switched off. This means any attempts to dismantle them is an attack on your own psychological make-up. **You are literally fighting yourself.**

So this is what a wallflower is: someone who feels shut behind a wall, often in the dark and alone, whilst on the other side of the wall the sun shines brightly and everyone is playing and enjoying themselves. The wallflower longs to be on the other side of the wall with everyone else, to drink in the sunshine and to know that the world is a great place to be, a place where they can flourish and where they have something significant to give to the world. The place that the wallflower longs for is where the sunflower lives.

## The original wallflowers

Very sadly a wallflower has become a derogatory term so that no one wants to be named or seen as a wallflower by other people. The term was used in the 19th century to describe a woman who attended dances, and who stood on the sidelines and either was not invited or declined any invitations to dance.

She was perceived as a lonely and sometimes unpopular figure, who appeared to prefer blending in with the background to taking part, and who chose to remain silent rather than engaging with others. Such women often lacked the skill to attract potential husbands and therefore spent the rest of their lives as spinsters, dependent on their families and stigmatised for their failure to function in normal life

## Wallflowers as a modern phenomenon

Fortunately we are no longer living in times when wallflowers were stigmatised in this way, yet more and more people are feeling like wallflowers or feel other people are seeing them like this. There are a number of factors that contribute to the creation of the wallflower as a modern phenomenon.

We are becoming an increasingly head-based society, with the emphasis on left-brain functioning as we progressively move through the digital age. We have been educated from an early age to operate principally from our analytical mind, to the detriment of the vastly superior emotional intelligence that lies in our natural intuition. Those working on computers day-in and day-out, and in sterile working environments, can also find themselves numbed by the negative ions that are constantly being pumped into their system. They become more and more head orientated as the computer requires them to put their thoughts into writing instead of verbally communicating them; as a result emotions and energy become depressed and then they wonder why they feel so depleted.

On top of this, there is the growing popularity of electronic communication that is having a significant impact on socialisation skills for many people, who are finding it harder and harder to communicate verbally. If feeling awkward, it's only too easy to dive into your phone and to appear busily preoccupied, rather than meet another person's gaze or strike up a conversation. Wallflowers are far more comfortable with texting, writing emails, surfing the Internet, listening to music, watching the world go round whilst they safely sit on the sidelines, protected from the attention of others. It's the wallflower's first love to be observing what other people are doing without any pressure to participate.

Approximately a third of the UK population are introverts (in some countries this proportion is much higher), who are generally quieter people, and as our culture becomes increasingly influenced by American values, more and more introverts are being pressured, even expected to behave more like extroverts. Currently, there is tremendous pressure to participate in the workplace, where there is an expectation to be to be visible; to be "out there"; to be a skilled networker; to contribute in meetings and break-out sessions; to deliver presentations; to be a great team-player and to be socially active with your colleagues. Most introverts struggle with this, or with some aspects of being in the spotlight, and many find a way to avoid these situations. A few lucky ones find a way to thrive in these conditions. However, many just feel inept and disadvantaged because they are unable to operate in the way they feel they ought to, and as a result they feel increasingly sidelined. No wonder many of them are now calling themselves wallflowers.

On top of all the challenges that social situations pose for quieter people, in the digital age there are increased pressures to be on social media, to demonstrate that you are popular by having thousands of friends on Facebook, to reveal yourself and personal facts about your life – yet without any real human contact. There is less and less real relating or real communication. Therefore, without practice, relating to others becomes increasingly difficult.

Elaine Aron reframed the experience for quiet, shy and reserved people in her book *The Highly Sensitive Person,* in which she normalised the experience of sensitivity. Sensitive children are more prone to bullying and being stigmatised for their sensitivity to the world around them, which leads to them developing avoidant behaviour and being labelled as wallflowers, shy, anti-social, or just plain weird. Sensitive people are highly sensitive to this kind of labelling, which increases the impact of it upon them.

All these factors contribute to the wallflower as a modern phenomenon and a product of the way our Western society works, creating exclusion, self-consciousness, isolation and difference.

**Men as wallflowers**

Although the original wallflowers were classically female, in current times wallflowers also include men, as evidenced by *The Perks of Being a Wallflower,* a book and film featuring a male protagonist. In the nineteenth century, there was no social stigma for men who refrained from dancing and/or participating socially. Such men were perceived as refined, dignified and enigmatic: the modern equivalent of "cool", because they stood back and observed, even if in actuality they were shy or reserved.

However, in the 21st century, more and more men are defining themselves as wallflowers because they have quieter personalities, or are introverts, or are highly sensitive. Although the softer qualities of men are valued, there are even greater expectations on men to perform and to **be everything**. As a result such men may feel acutely at a disadvantage, and that they are perceived by others as being un- masculine or lacking in some fundamental way. They may find it hard to socialise and to meet some of their professional obligations, and therefore may be overlooked for promotion, even though they may be highly skilled and capable in many key areas. (This is, of course, experienced by women too - but can have a deeper impact on male confidence.) Men may also find it hard to form romantic relationships because of the pressure on them, even in this day and age, to initiate romantic connections.

If you've seen an interview with Stephen Chbosky, author and director of *The Perks of Being a Wallflower* who in his younger years identified as a wallflower, you may have noticed there is nothing un- masculine about him. Thus, it's really important as a man that you value your qualities of sensitivity, listening and observing, and find ways of using them to your advantage. Some of the most powerful and successful men in the contemporary world are quiet, reserved and introverted, and may have battled with many of things that you do. However, they have found a way of overcoming their challenges and developing their positive aspects, so their apparent disadvantages have actually become assets. This is your challenge, and I hope the material in this book will help you to see yourself in a different light, whatever gender you are.

## About this book

If you think this is a book about flowers, you are mistaken. This is a book about courageous people: courageous and sensitive people, often with significant abilities, who are trapped within themselves.

They are both and women at all stages of life, as you will be discovering in the personal stories within this book.

Most books and advice handed out on confidence may work very well for certain people – but they don't work for wallflowers. This is because most confidence-building techniques don't address the complex psychological process that is keeping you locked behind powerful internal walls, and this is why so many of them only have short-term benefits. In fact, there is a missing link, and without that link it's going to be harder to access the natural confidence that lives within you. I happened on it by chance, which enabled me to end my wallflower experience in a few short months. And as I was later to discover, I had hit on the same way that had enabled countless famous ex-wallflowers do the same.

Much later, I developed the Sunflower Effect, bringing ancient and modern confidence-building methods together. This is the missing link, that has enabled several thousand people to move out from behind their wall and find their inner "sunflower" - the confident person that lies hidden within them. Some of these never believed that this would ever be possible and had given up all hope that they could ever change.

I will be using the terms "wallflower" and "sunflower" as a metaphor for what goes on inside you internally, so you can understand your inner workings better. I will also give you tools to change your situation. The metaphor "from wallflower to sunflower" also acts a bridge for you to move from the invisible place of the wallflower through claiming your inner sunflower: the part of you that has the potential to shine. In time, you will find the momentum to move across the fast moving River of Life to where the sunflowers live, and become the person you've always wanted to be. You will do this effortlessly and in your own way. It won't even think about it because it will be a natural process, as natural to you as walking or jumping. You will be your own sunflower, not a replica of every other sunflower. You won't have a fake confidence where you are hiding your insecurities (which is the experience of many so-called confident people). You will be truly yourself: confident in your own way. This is your birthright and the person you were always meant to be.

The book includes some personal sharing from my own life, which I hope will inspire you to take action, so you too can make the transition from wallflower to sunflower. When I started out I had very low expectations of what I could achieve, and I had no grand plans. I had no inkling that the very thing that was so excruciatingly painful to me was going to be the passage to my greatest freedom. Not only that, it was going to bring me a fulfilment in life that was way beyond my deepest dreams.

As the book proceeds, we will develop an intimate relationship through which you will have the opportunity to get to know and understand yourself better. The book will serve as our meeting point, and I write it with this in mind: not as a treatise on all the wisdom I have acquired over the last forty years, but as a personal relationship between us in which a process of transformation can occur. I will therefore often be speaking to you as if you were here in the room with me. It cannot be the same as if we were working together physically, but the distance can be to our advantage. It can serve as a starting place and give you time and space to prepare yourself for the change you want to see in your life. For as you read you will be processing many thoughts, feelings and experiences, and through this you will be opening up your own way forward. This is the most important function of the book.

**I'm not going to say it's easy.** Saying goodbye permanently to the wallflower is complex and not an easy thing to achieve. If you've tried you will know this. However, it can be much easier that you would think. It will take commitment, determination, and perseverance. You will face many challenges, and at times you won't believe that you can do it, but if you persist you will gradually overcome all these. Many people walk into one of my courses and walk out a completely new person, as if they have shed an old skin and have discovered a sparkly new one underneath. In fact, that sparkly skin was always there; it was just waiting for you to discover it.

The ease with which you will be able to do shed your wallflower identity depends a lot on your personality and some of the experiences you've had in your life. But even people with very difficult situations have managed to make a profound shift in their confidence levels, and as a result changed how they feel about themselves and their lives. Once that shift has taken place, more shifts inevitably follow.

### How to make faster progress

As you read this book, you will get to know what has made the most difference in moving me from wallflower to sunflower. Believe me, I have faced many challenges, including huge resistance, fear, lots of disappointments and setbacks. It took me many years to reach the place that I am in now. So one of the intentions of this book is to make this process **much faster for you.**

I will be outlining the pitfalls that you may encounter, so you will have a way of dealing with them, and can **get back on track as fast as possible.** I suggest you keep a notebook beside you, because I will be giving you exercises as you go along, which will take your processing journey deeper. It's also helpful to jot down any ideas, thoughts or memories that might be stimulated. Writing can be a powerful way of processing your experience; so don't underestimate its usefulness.

Success is a two-pronged fork: the first is changing your mindset and the second is changing your behaviour. If you change your behaviour without changing your mindset, you will find it very hard to sustain your newfound behaviour. This is how destructive your own mind can be, as you will discover later on. If you change your mindset without changing your behaviour, you will feel good for a while, but without any change of behaviour you will find yourself creeping back into your old ways of thinking and being.

You will have the opportunity to participate in a number of exercises so you can also participate at an experiential level, which will take you much deeper into your inner workings, and make this book far more effective. From time to time, I will be inviting you to visit the www.fromwallflowertosunflower.com website, where you can download the bonuses and other resources.

A book on its own cannot bring about the radical change you are seeking. No book can, since it's operating through words and concepts, which will keep you in your analytical mind. It's going to have a very hard job shifting you in areas where you have a lot of repressed emotion or trauma, which most wallflowers acquire as a result of their experiences. This is why it's so important to actually participate in the exercises, because this will enable you to also to work at an experiential level with the deeper causes that have been keeping you a wallflower. You will be working with your **inner theatre** and the countless characters that live inside your head; often these internal characters are in conflict and causing you enormous stress and suffering. You will be working with some of these inner characters in order to bring them out into the open and over time put an end to this conflict.

The bonuses and exercises will turn a short book into a much more powerful transformation machine. Some of these bonuses will give you access to private videos, audios and documents that are only accessible to you as a reader of this book.

## Your way forward

Everyone's journey is individual and unique, and what suits one does not suit another. The role of this book is to stimulate you to discover your own truth so you can find **your own way forward**. Thus, if something in the book doesn't resonate for you, put it aside. Maybe you will come back to it, or maybe another thread will draw you. From my experience, it's often the ideas that come completely out of the blue and that arrive unexpectedly in your awareness, that are the valuable ones. This is what this book is **seeking to develop in you.**

In the book, I will also be explaining complex psychological theory in a way that I hope will make it easier to grasp. It's actually not as simplistic as this, but I hope these explanations will enable you to understand some of the principles that underlie the Sunflower Effect. However, it's not important for you to understand the theory in order to gain benefit from the practice.

In the next chapter, you will discover the secret that has enabled countless famous ex-wallflowers to achieve lasting confidence and how you can start taking the first steps to shedding your wallflower identity. You will have the opportunity to participate in a powerful exercise that, if you put it into practice, will almost guarantee your long-term success, particularly if you can find a way to follow the path I am outlining in this book.

## Chapter 2

# The Secret of the Stars

**The secret that ex-wallflower movie stars know about (and most people don't) that enabled them to fulfil their dreams**

Every time I switch on the radio, I hear an actor, a movie star, a comedian, a singer, a public figure telling the same story - that they used to be quiet, shy, a wallflower or avoided the spotlight. Then one day all that changed, and they were able to overcome their inhibitions. It's usually pretty much the same solution, and the same thing that enabled me to put an end to my wallflower existence and put me on the path to becoming the person I am today.

The secret of how we did this has actually been known for years - some wallflowers were deliberately thrown from frying pan into the fire, with the hope that they would shake off their reticence and blossom into confident adults. They were sent to performing arts classes, or they found themselves in a situation where they were required to perform.

For those it worked for, it was an extremely successful strategy. My mother often told stories from her school days about Dorothy Tutin, then a quiet and reserved girl, who was sent to RADA to bring her out. It worked and she went onto to become one of the most important actresses of her age. Others went on to become great speakers; or they excelled in the performing arts; or they became great leaders, innovators, or founded organisations that had a great impact on the world. Most went on to live the life and become the person they always wanted to be, that at one time had seemed so far beyond their reach. See this book's website for examples of famous ex-wallflowers who made this radical change to their lives.

However, for those it didn't work for, it may have lead to even greater reticence, even greater reason to avoid the spotlight and a catalogue of excruciating memories that they have no wish to ever repeat. There is so much more to moving from wallflower to sunflower than simply getting up on stage. The conditions have to right - this is what this book is all about.

I will be unfolding how I did it, even though I had almost zero self- belief and very low expectations of what I could accomplish. This is true for the several thousand reserved men and women who have experienced the Sunflower Effect and almost effortlessly said goodbye to their wallflower identity. This is the missing link, as I mentioned in Chapter 1 that will enable you to achieve the same.

## Motivation to change

Sometimes the transition from wallflower to sunflower happened by chance for these famous ex-wallflowers, but for many, it came from a very strong motivation to make a change to their situation. They had got to the point where **they couldn't stand being a wallflower any longer** - they knew they had something within them that they **just had to get out**. It had just got too uncomfortable and painful to hide themselves away any longer.

As result, they reached deep into themselves and took the plunge. Although their first attempts may have been inept, when they stepped out from behind the sidelines, they discovered their fear of expressing themselves was often much greater than the actuality, and that other people were only too glad to welcome them. Over time their wallflower existence simply melted away. If you feel strong motivation, you can achieve similar breakthroughs too.

### What if I don't have the motivation?

What if you don't feel strong motivation? What if you don't feel strongly about anything? Or what if you doubt your capacity to sustain motivation over a period of time because of the many disappointments, setbacks and traumas you have had?

This is the point. You probably don't feel strong motivation because of all those disheartening experiences. I was just the same. This is part of the problem and what is keeping you on the sidelines. Many of the famous ex-wallflowers experienced this too. There were many times that they doubted they could make it. But they found a way to keep going despite the disappointment and the failures; and to keep believing that they could change if they kept at it long enough. You may have heard the story of the injured ex-paratrooper who gained so much weight that he could barely walk; he actually needed a wheelchair to get around. This man started doing yoga, and at first he could barely do one of the basic poses. Even as he progressed, holding his balance was very difficult - he fell many, many times. But he said to himself: *"Just because I can't do it today, doesn't mean I'm not going to be able to do it SOME day."*

It became his mantra. Not only did he lose an enormous amount of weight, achieve body control and personal fitness - he could also run. And running for him was the fullest expression of his success. This was his sunflower experience. Knowing he had achieved this, gave him enormous confidence and pride in himself. His story now inspires thousands on YouTube and you can see it on this book's website.

Do you want to stay stuck a wallflower or are you willing to take the first small step? That's all it will take. When Neil Armstrong took his first step on the moon, he took a giant leap for mankind. When you take your first step, you take a giant leap for your life. It doesn't matter what happens as a result of that first step. Whether you succeed or fail - the important thing is that **you did it.** If you keep doing it, your wallflower identity will gradually dissolve. (Funny enough, Neil Armstrong was a quiet, retiring man who found himself playing a very big part in world history. He demonstrated that being quiet and retiring doesn't need to stop you.)

## The power of commitment

**Nothing happens without commitment,** without calling forth the power of intention. This is what enabled the ex-wallflowers to turn into radiant sunflowers and the ex-paratrooper to achieve the impossible. Even if your commitment might waver, articulating your commitment as an intention is powerful. It sets a momentum in process, which will make achieving your goal so much easier.

Deepak Chopra, Wayne Dyer and many other authors have demonstrated just how powerful it is to work with intention. It will enable you to achieve goals that have been unreachable up to now. You will find their books on this book's website, along with other books I recommend.

This is why I **distinguish between an intention and a goal** or any other kind of resolution or promise that you make to yourself. If you don't achieve your goal, then you will feel disappointed with yourself, and you may start punishing yourself for your failure to achieve what you set out to do. Most goals are time-limited, with a fixed end-time when it's expected the goal will be achieved. This is fine for some of the things you want to achieve, where there are clear stages and tasks. All you need to do is to create a strategy, apply yourself to the tasks, and keep going until your goal is accomplished. You may have setbacks but you can still achieve your goal, if you stick with it.

However, with something as nebulous and complex as moving from wallflower to sunflower, you can't tick the steps off as you would items on a shopping list. Confidence has a tendency to move in swings and roundabouts. There may also be unseen internal obstacles that block progress. Sometimes it can feel that you are swimming against the tide when actually you are making headway. And it's often very hard to judge progress. When you hit an obstacle, this may actually be huge progress because your internal defense system has been triggered and you are now working with the deeper blocks to your confidence. However, your negative mind sees this as failure. It tells you that you're not confident in the way you want to be, in spite of all your efforts, so you might as well give up hope of it ever changing.

This is the difference between setting a goal and setting an intention. An intention is an **ongoing activity.** So long as you are committed to your intention, it will continue to empower you to achieving your objective. Any failure or setback is all part of the process, and not a reason to give up. It may take a few hours to achieve your intention or it may take several years, depending on the nature of the intention. For those **really big** intentions, it may take the whole of your life. It doesn't matter how long it takes. What's important is that you commit to your intention and keep faith that you will achieve it in time.

Your doubts, fears, resistance and any obstacles you encounter are all part of the process and, as I will be demonstrating in the rest of this book, they are an essential part of the process of moving from wallflower to sunflower. The obstacles are there for a reason and are an aspect of your internal defense system. Overcoming your doubts, fears and resistance are steps along the path.

## Exercise – making a commitment

This brings us to this powerful exercise - making a commitment to the journey and **setting a powerful intention** so you can achieve your objective with ease. You may want to read through the next section and get an overview of the whole exercise so you know what to expect.

But first you may want to claim Bonus 1, which will increase the effectiveness of the exercise for you. I highly recommend you take advantage of this free resource by visiting this book's website: www.fromwallflowertosunflower.com and signing up for all 4 of my free Bonuses.

## BONUS 1 Making the commitment exercise even more powerful.

There is nothing quite like receiving support and encouragement. It's one of the key features of the Sunflower Effect (see Witnessing in Chapter 6). Right now I can only give you that support by technological means, but it can be as effective as if we were really in the room together. Your imagination is a very powerful tool, particularly when it's combined with emotion. I will be explaining how this works later on in the book.

**Bonus 1 includes:**

- An MP3 recording of the exercise so you don't have to look at written instructions and will be able to experience the exercise at a far deeper level. If you listen to this through headphones, it will go right into the limbic system of your brain, which activates your fear and resistance to change. In time this will help you to dissolve these negative effects.

- A PDF of your pact, which you can fill out and sign and keep as physical evidence of the commitment you have made. We will be referring to this throughout this book.

- A video of me witnessing your signed pact, and offering you support and encouragement. You can come back any time to this video and receive support and acknowledgment from me: particularly when you are hitting a bad patch or needing a boost. This will help you to keep going through the challenging times and increase your chances of long-term success.

## Exercise: From wallflower to sunflower - making your commitment

**Step 1 Preparation**

Start by gently closing your eyes, and just taking a moment for yourself. Take some deep breaths, breathing deep into your belly. This is where your emotions lie. Just take some time to notice what is there and how it feels inside you. Notice where you are holding tension in your body. Are you clenching your jaw, tensing your stomach, shoulders or neck? Notice it and then, in your own time, invite the tension to relax. Just let it all go. If it doesn't want to release, that's OK. Just be with it.

**Step 2 Your deepest wish**

And now, as you breathe, allow yourself to enter into your deepest wish for yourself. Maybe it was the impetus that caused you to buy this book, or maybe it's something that has been milling around in your awareness forever. Just let yourself experience that wish. Truly experience how it feels. Perhaps you will see images of yourself in the future, or have a sense of how you would like to feel. Even more powerful is to imagine you have already achieved your wish. Notice how it feels when you truly claim this experience for yourself as a present reality.

**Step 3 Being Witnessed**

Now see me sitting across from you: I too am wishing the very best for you, and for you to find fulfilment and freedom. Together we are going to make a pact. The pact is a commitment to following-through on whatever it might take and however long it might take, to make that wish into a reality. It's a pact that is binding, not in the sense of being restrictive but in the sense of keeping the faith and holding on to what will truly bring you fulfilment. Breathe into that pact: feel it and make it real for yourself. Invite helpers to come forward to make the journey easier, and the openness to recognise them when they come along. Remain here as long as you need to truly integrate the pact into your deeper self, so that you are clear as to what it is - and that you are willing to commit to it.

**Step 4 Recording your pact**

When you are ready, gently open your eyes and write down your pact, either on the PDF provided in Bonus 1 or on a clean piece of paper. Then sign and date it. Like any legal document, this pact is binding. Do not sign it unless you are sure you are willing to stand by it, no matter what challenges come your way: there may be many.

Remember this is about intention. Keeping the intention alive and your commitment to it, is all that is required.

**Step 5 Reinforcement**

Look at this pact often to remind yourself of the commitment you have made. Breathe into the "energy" of your pact. In other words, notice how you feel when you read through your pact. See yourself achieving these things effortlessly and easily.

You have started on a powerful journey, which will move you from wallflower to sunflower. The last chapter of this book will explain the stages in the journey and will include some guidance on how to get you through the challenges and pitfalls.

In the next two chapters, I will describe my journey from wallflower to sunflower and what made the most difference to me. You will also be discovering how to avoid the biggest mistake that wallflowers make when they are trying to become sunflowers.

## Chapter 3

# The Making of the Wallflower

**The biggest mistake that wallflowers make when they're trying to build confidence**

As far back as I can remember I was always a wallflower, always on the sidelines and avoiding attention. I was a cling-to-the edges kind of child, and this continued way beyond normal childhood reticence. When I was three and my mother took me to a mother-and-child movement class: I refused to participate and stayed at the side of the room. After many attempts to get me to take part (an activity that I now love), my mother gave up. This unwillingness to participate in groups became my *modus operandi*.

On my first day at school, I sat for the whole day on the teacher's lap, too terrified to leave it. It was made clear that I couldn't sit there every day, so I kept to the edges of the room, a shy and unusually good child who was seen but not heard. This was a feature of my schooldays from then on, and even my teachers registered that there was something unnerving about my immaculately good behaviour. Badges were awarded weekly within each class to encourage achievement. They didn't have a G badge for being good; they did, however, have two special heart shaped badges, P for politeness and K for kindness. Whilst other children got A for arithmetic and E for English, I inevitably received the

Kindness and Politeness badges, week in and week out. I didn't have to do anything to earn them - it was just who and what I was.

There were all kinds of reasons for this unnerving good behaviour. I was an unexpected early arrival in my parents' relationship and by chance, they had chosen a flat where the landlady felt it incumbent to inform my mother that her baby was crying. My mother, being only too aware of this fact, discovered that if she put me in the bathroom, the easily disturbed landlady could not hear my crying. It must have seemed like a simple solution. Much later when I finally sought the help of a therapist, I discovered that I had absorbed the message that crying/self-expression lead to banishment, so I avoided any behaviour that might repeat this experience. Unconsciously I believed that self-expression was bad.

## An affinity for walls

I had developed an affinity for walls; it seems, from early on. When I was very young, my father was painting the walls of our flat and he, no doubt, was afraid I would ruin his good work so he would repeatedly cry out, *"Mind the walls and doors!"* For a small child this was terrifying, as my father was very tall and his voice rather loud. He was rather fond of this phrase and he continued to call it out intermittently right into my teenage years. Although I can't remember the original occasion, every time I heard it my body registered a kind of panic. The fact that my father thought it was all a huge joke added to my confusion.

Staying close to the walls was where I felt safe - I didn't like being in the middle of the room, or anywhere I could be seen and noticed. Every time I ventured into that territory, I felt a terror, possibly the terror of a young child who was afraid of where she should be in the room and couldn't be sure of where she was safe.

## Seen but not heard

Then when I was four my parents moved to a bigger flat, where the residents association of the flats disliked children. My parents regularly received complaints about the noisy kids, even to the extent of solicitors' letters and the erection of barbed wire so we wouldn't play in the gardens. Once again my sister and I were kept under restraint. Thus emerged two children who developed the art of playing quietly and avoiding adult attention.

Was this misfortune? Was I a victim? Did the same kind of things happen to you, and maybe much worse things? Terrible things? Somehow you survived, you got through. **You adapted.** In my case, when I look back on it, it almost felt like a conspiracy. Almost as if it was my destiny to experience these things for some bigger purpose. Much later, at a turning point in my life, this and almost everything else I had experienced began to make sense.

## Being a scapegoat

At my first school, the teacher of my class had created the Learner Seat, derived from the number of learner drivers that drove up and down the road outside my school. The seat had a driving "L" tied to the back of the chair. As I was quiet and didn't speak up and also a bit of a dreamer, I found myself in the Learner Seat most of the time. I knew it was bad and I believed I was stupid. The more I believed I was stupid, the more afraid I was of making mistakes; the more I made mistakes, the more afraid I was of everything, and the more trapped I became.

The girl behind me continually kicked my seat when the teacher wasn't looking. The existence of the Learner Seat, designed to encourage the other children to work hard, gave permission for other children to abuse and exclude me. I believed I was stupid because the teacher said I was, and other children kicked me because the teacher had branded me as the one that was lagging behind everyone else. But I wasn't stupid; I was just quiet and so overwhelmed by the teaching methods that I felt a failure most of the time - so I failed. It was a self-fulfilling prophecy. So I did everything I could to avoid being seen. I concealed myself - so no one would notice me - so I wouldn't be excluded in the future.

Most people grow up with a terror of being seen as stupid, because they know they will be rejected and stigmatised by others. If you have had similar experiences you probably have developed a strategy for coping with this, as I did. In psychology this is called the "scapegoat" - one who is seen as being different from everyone else. Every primitive society had a scapegoat, and they were often seen as a threat to that society and driven out. They were undesirable; because the fear was that their existence weakened that society and its ability to survive.

Whilst the sophistication of our modern society means we don't need to drive out the scapegoat, the patterns still exist in human behaviour. Psychology recognises it and sees it being played out in almost any group - in teams, departments, clubs, classes, schools, colleges, universities, committees, working parties, gangs, friendships, and particularly in families. It's potentially in any place where people come together. The group operates fine for a while until something happens and then one person is blamed because they are perceived as weaker; or because they are sensitive; or less able to defend themselves; or less adept at playing social games.

This process happens in groups too, where people are trying to overcome these negative effects – self-help groups, women's groups, men's groups, support groups, therapy groups etc. This is why it's important that members of the group are aware of their power to scapegoat one another. Naming it dissolves these effects and brings the group together.

When I was eight, we moved from the constricted environment to a house where we had far more freedom, but I was to be scapegoated once more. It was the sixties, the heyday of the Beatles, and on my first day in my new school I was asked if I liked the Beatles. I didn't know who the Beatles were but my parents, being old- fashioned, saw the Beatles as a bad thing. So, with no other knowledge, I trotted out my parents' opinions, ignorant that this was going to produce another kind of isolation.

I was "sent to Coventry" and ignored by the whole school. No one would speak to me - I could feel the dislike and disapproval of these "nice" middle-class children. Luckily the two ugliest girls in the school were also excluded and so the three of us made the best of it. But we all knew we were misfits and avoided. My scapegoating days ended when that school closed and, as parents removed their children to other schools, one child who had lost all her friends approached me. She asked me if I really did like the Beatles, and I knew by then to say, "Yes."

The legacy of all this meant that I continuously sought adult approval and generally felt more comfortable with adults than other children because they were less likely to scapegoat me. But I also feared adults and their power to ridicule me as my first teacher had. Thus I was stuck; I couldn't really trust adults, even though most were more reliable than other children. I was always walking a tightrope and any minute I could find myself sprawling on the floor.

A little later when I was at another school, I was so terrified of authority and so afraid to speak up that I was unable to tell the teacher I really needed to go to the bathroom. This teacher was very strict about this and wanted to encourage her pupils to stay in the classroom for the whole lesson, but my discomfort was getting unbearable. Finally, I had no choice but to let go, and I cried out, "Look, I'm all wet," pretending that the wetness had come from a magical source. Of course, everyone knew I had wet my pants. I was already well experienced in other children branding me as a misfit, and that's what I expected them to do, even though these children were a lot kinder than those at my other school.

## Becoming a near-saint

The only thing I knew what to do was to be "good." A girl in my class who was a Roman Catholic and was studying saints had asked the headmistress if there was anyone in the school who was a saint. The headmistress, who also was our class teacher, said there were no saints in the school but there was one "near-saint." The girl puzzled as to whom this "near-saint" could be and finally she decided it must be me.

After that, I was always the "near-saint" in her eyes, and she continually referred to me that way. It was rather nice to be heralded as a "near-saint," even if only by one person; better than being the "stupid one." It made me feel special. Saints, after all, were exemplary people, but I also began to wonder was I too good, too nice, too kind?

## Being expected to speak up

As my school days went on, it became clear that being good, nice and kind were not enough. We were expected to speak up for ourselves, to express our opinions, to participate; otherwise, we were considered stupid. However, on the one occasion when I had begun to express myself, the whole class was going a bit crazy and the headmistress walked in. The first person she saw was me, the good girl, the "near saint". If I was going crazy, then she really had problems. She grabbed me and spoke some harsh words. I was immediately shamed into submission. Inside myself I made a decision: as soon as I express myself, I am punished. It was the same message I had received over and over again.

Thus, when I was expected to express myself, I simply couldn't. I was the quiet one, the girl that wouldn't say "boo" to a goose, the wallflower who kept to the edges of the room, and I only moved away from them when I was sure that no one would attack or shame me. Speaking up involved a possibility of being ridiculed and I was afraid of getting it wrong in case I was seen as stupid.

The less I spoke, the less I was expected to speak. People simply ignored me. I became invisible, and gradually I retreated more and more into my shell, almost to a point of feeling that I didn't really exist. If a teacher called out my name, I almost jumped out of my skin, because I didn't believe I could be seen. This made it worse because I realised that my invisibility was highly visible to others who were just choosing to ignore me.

A little later I acquired teenage spots, which gave me even more reasons to hide away. All I could see was the horrible spots on my face and I believed that I was ugly, just at the time when it was important to look attractive. Other girl spent hours in the toilets preening themselves, whilst I did everything I could to avoid looking in the mirror because I didn't want to be faced with the ugliness of my spots. I felt more and more different from other girls, who I saw as the sunflowers: the popular ones, the attractive ones, the ones that everyone felt drawn to. I felt drawn to them too but I believed they would never like me or choose me as a friend. I began to fear them. I believed that I could never be like them. I would always be a wallflower stuck on the sidelines.

## Powerful decisions

If you are resonating with some aspects of my story, you may also be aware, like me, of the decisions that you made at the time about yourself, and the strategy you developed to cope with it. This is what everyone does. Sometimes those decisions are positive and help to build your confidence and self-esteem, and are usually as a result of positive experiences. But when those decisions are negative, they create powerful blocks to your confidence.

This is the "Chimp" at work. The Chimp is a very primitive part of our brain described by Dr Steve Peters in his book *The Chimp Paradox* (which I highly recommend) that makes simplistic decisions based on the evidence at the time. As those decisions become reinforced through life experiences, they begin to acquire immense power.

## The biggest mistake wallflowers make when they are trying to build confidence

One of the most powerful decisions that many wallflowers make is looking around at the confident people, the sunflowers, believing that they HAVE IT ALL and that, as a result, all kinds of advantages are heaped on them that don't come to wallflowers? This pattern followed me into adulthood, in which I believed that everything was set up for the confident ones, who I saw as having "a silver spoon in their mouth". I believed that they were always going to be one step ahead of me because that's the "law of the jungle."

You may like me have similar beliefs based on plenty of evidence. You see certain people climbing the career ladder more easily than anyone else. They take risks and rarely fall flat on their faces and, if they do, they're witty and quick thinking and they find some way of recovering from the situation without anyone noticing that they made a boo-boo. They're people persons and they always seem to know what to say in any situation. Everyone seems to like them because they have a way of not only being confident, but also everyone seeks them out for advice or help when they're facing a crisis. Because they trust this person, they know that they will never let them down.

Instead, what do you experience? Other people telling you you're not confident enough, you need to be more social, speak up more, be more assertive and believe in yourself more – in short, behave more like the confident people do. **And that's where you're stuck.**

Either you simply can't do any of these things, or when you do stick your neck out; do what everyone keeps telling you; do what all the books tell you - then you fall flat on your face. You get tongue-tied; or you panic and it comes out all wrong; or you just don't manage to grab their full attention. And then the other person (or group) cuts you down with a look, a few terse words, or don't get what you're saying. Even worse, when someone else steals your thunder, says exactly what you've just said. Except they say it with confidence and conviction and then get all the credit **for your idea.**

If you've had just a few of these experiences, it would go without saying that you would feel daunted by the prospect of repeating them. If this has happened many, many times, then you will have powerful proof that sticking your neck out doesn't work for someone like you and, if anyone tells you again what you **should be doing** and then judges you for not making the effort, you'd love to strangle them for their well-meaning but patronising advice!

These experiences are the making of the wallflower, and the reason why many people feel there is no way out. Staying on the sidelines is really the only option, so you might as well make the best of it since nothing is ever going to change.

However, this is the BIGGEST MISTAKE that most wallflowers make when they're trying to build confidence.

## It all started in the playground

It's not surprising you think like this. For many wallflowers, it all started in the playground and it's been reinforced ever since. In the playground there were certain children that were able to be more expressive and participated fully in whatever activity was going on; and there were others that held back or just preferred quieter activities and were seen as different. Because children have under- developed brains and haven't yet learned compassion for others, they can be very cruel, particularly when they see others behaving differently. If those other children appear to be retreating, this can bring out some very primitive responses. If you've been on the receiving end of this, it can leave very deep scars, which may have caused you to make powerful decisions about who you are and your place in the world.

If this didn't happen in childhood, it may have happened at some other time in some other way that resulted in similar beliefs about yourself in relation to other people. Shakespeare declared that "All the world's a stage" with the leading actors taking prime positions centre stage and in the spotlight, whilst others find themselves off to the side or towards the back of the stage, supporting the main action but rarely getting to take their place in the spotlight. Even worse are those perpetually waiting in the wings, who never get the chance to participate on the Stage of Life. For most people, this means that there is one group of people who have more advantages and other people that don't - one group of people who succeed and others that don't.

## Bonus 2 Exercise: Powerful Decisions

### Reversing the decisions that made you into a wallflower

I have created a powerful bonus to enable you to identify and dispel the powerful decisions that you made at an earlier stage in your life. It's going to help you to say goodbye to your wallflower identity for good. I suggest you do the exercise in Bonus 2 right now. This is something that you can be working with, on an ongoing basis, so you can notice when these decisions surface and make a new decision. If you haven't yet downloaded the book's bonuses simply visit this book's website.

In the next chapter, you will be learning how I happened by chance on the same secret that had enabled the famous ex-wallflowers to put an end to their wallflower experience - often in a surprisingly short amount of time.

## Chapter 4

# The End of the Wallflower

**How I put an end to my wallflower existence and changed my prospects in a matter of a few short months**

It was by pure chance that I ended my time as a wallflower and started my new life as a sunflower. This took the form of a series of events and coincidences, none particularly significant on their own, which led to a dramatic shift in my prospects.

Shyness had followed me into adulthood and as a quiet girl with few expectations of what my life could be, I was halfway through a nursing training. Nursing had appealed as a rewarding career path, which would not make too many demands on my Good Girl role. However, I was a square peg in a round hole, ill suited to the profession and far from happy. The work was hard to cope with, emotionally stressful and I alternated between periods of ill-health and depression. Deep inside I was desperate to escape.

**A lifeline**

Then one day Life threw me a lifeline. I was working in the casualty department and whilst I was in between patients, the most attractive and popular doctor walked into the clinical room and found me reading Franz Kafka. He enquired why I was doing nursing when, quite plainly (to him), I should be doing an English Literature degree.

"Oh no, I couldn't do that," I replied, "I'm not nearly clever enough."

I hated to tell him that I hadn't got a particularly good grade in my English Literature A Level. But he had hit on a deep dream - I would have loved to be doing an English Literature degree but I doubted in my abilities to be accepted on a course.

"Of course you could," he said and walked off, unaware of the impact that he was making on me.

If he had been anyone else I probably wouldn't have taken much notice – but he was the most desirable doctor in the department and had bothered to take the time to talk to me, even if I was far too shy to speak to him. No doubt he saw I was a bit of a wallflower, but kind of interesting since I was reading Franz Kafka - not the easiest of authors to read at age 20. Perhaps he saw there was a spark in me that I wasn't aware of. I never saw him again, so I never had an opportunity to thank him for encouraging me to dare to live my dream.

After that I began to form a resolve that I would leave nursing and do a degree in English Literature, or at least give it a try. Even if I failed, I was taking some positive step to follow a path that would bring me more happiness and fulfilment.

**KEY POINT: Are other people telling you that you should do things you don't think you can do?**

Perhaps you have had similar experiences. Do other people have far more faith in your abilities than you have? Jot these down in your notebook. Every time someone suggests another career or avenue for you, or comments on something you're good at, jot it down. Maybe they see something in you that you can't see or aren't ready to see at the moment. Each one of these is a lifeline. Is Destiny knocking on your door because it has other plans for you, but you are unable to hear?

Whether you believe in Destiny or the existence of a Higher Power, it doesn't matter; the fact is that other people are seeing a potential in you that is calling out to be expressed. **Listen to them.**

## My road to Damascus

Some time later, Life once more intervened and I was shown a new pathway. Funnily enough it was my body that produced the first symptoms of my deep unhappiness – and opened up the pathway that would eventually enable me to escape from the roles and behaviours that were keeping me stuck. I was suffering from a number of symptoms and my GP had misdiagnosed me with a gall bladder problem, unusual in one so young, and prescribed some tablets.

On the day of a fancy dress party that my flat-mates and I were arranging, I developed crippling pain, suspected to be a burst appendix. I was rushed into hospital and admitted to the nurses' ward. That night the night nurse on duty was a student at RADA who was supplementing her income by doing some agency nursing. We found we had a lot in common; she heard about my dissatisfaction with nursing and hope of going to university to study English Literature, whilst she infused me with her enthusiasm for her drama training. She was so alive and passionate about what she was doing that I began to seriously consider following a path to drama school. A hospital bed may be an unlikely place for a Road to Damascus but it was mine.

I had my friend bring the unread books of plays I had on bookshelves and I read them avidly. I couldn't wait to share my impressions with the night nurse when she came on duty. She was just as enthusiastic as I was about my new plan. The pain in my abdomen disappeared and a couple of days later I was discharged. The cause of the pain, the doctors suspected, was an allergy to the gall bladder tablets I had been prescribed and which, of course, I didn't need since there was nothing wrong with my gall bladder. The only thing wrong with me had been a dose of unhappiness that had produced the initial psychosomatic symptoms.

## A new direction

Now I had a new direction to follow. I became an enthusiastic theatre-goer. I was lucky enough to have the whole of the London stage to explore. I was blown away the first time I saw Ian McKellen perform. I can't even remember now what the play was, but his performance was spellbinding.

I became enamoured by every aspect of the theatre. I loved the atmosphere of the auditorium as I entered and took my seat. I loved all the velvet and gold of the old proscenium arch London theatres, the air thick with a denseness that seemed to wrap itself around me. I loved the feeling of anticipation before the play started, and then the magic created by lighting and costume. Then it was the wonder of being in the presence of the living and breathing actor, the powerful emotions expressed and how the actor could make me feel. It was absolutely real to me. I came out of the theatre feeling more alive than I could remember feeling, since the last time I was in a theatre. It was almost as if what had been expressed on the stage was more real to me than my own life. The artifice of the performance brought me to a level of awareness that I longed to experience. As much as I loved English Literature, drama was giving me something that a Victorian novel couldn't.

I signed up for a drama course during one of my holidays. I had such high hopes that this course would give me something of the experience that the nurse at RADA had described. However, the teacher was old-fashioned in her teaching methods, even for that time. She barked out orders, balling us out if we set off on our downstage foot instead of our upstage foot. It was a miserable experience and I came away from the course realising that I had had enough of people ordering me around. If this was what drama was then this wasn't for me, and I returned to my plan to study English Literature.

Actually it was a lucky escape. Drama school auditions would have been traumatic and I wasn't nearly ready, from what I know about how drama schools operated at that time, even if I'd got into one. The experience would have destroyed my fragile confidence.

Notice that it wasn't a smooth path for me. I made countless mistakes and took wrong paths too numerous to mention here. I hit obstacles, took stock and changed direction, even if it meant returning to an original plan. I was still on the right course and something inside me knew it.

## A powerful decision

When I finally went to university, and it took me several years to get there, I was determined to use a new place where no one knew me, to tackle my shyness head on. I was absolutely sick to death of living my life on the sidelines, seeing other people who were more comfortable with themselves, having fun and expressing themselves naturally. I was ready to climb out of my box. I knew I would have to reinvent myself: I would have to stop being the person that I had been. I have really given up on the idea of drama by then, but as luck would have it, I had chosen a university that was strong in drama. In Fresher's Week I went to a drama workshop run by the drama wing of the English Lit. Dept. and loved every minute of it. There was an active Theatre Group in the Students Union and the English Lit. Department had developed a strong Drama wing under the inspiring leadership of Philip Roberts that was turning out outstanding productions.

My very first performance on stage was terrifying. I had a very small part, playing a narrator. The theatre lights were dazzling but I could still see one of my tutors in one of the front rows. Somehow I got through it. I knew I hadn't been brilliant but I had made a start and much to my surprise I had enjoyed the thrill of being in front of that audience. I had felt incredible warmth from them. Every one of them, including my tutor, was smiling and wanted me to do well.

It was rather like the thrill of jumping off a high diving board, utterly terrifying but with the feeling of a great achievement. I had done something that I didn't think I could do, on top of the fact that I was now studying English Literature at a reputable university. I was beginning to break some of the old patterns and beliefs that had kept me stuck over so many years. I was doing things I really enjoyed and it was liberating me.

### Discovering the secret

I had discovered the secret that the ex-wallflower movie stars had hit on that had enabled them to break free of their self-consciousness. They found it in acting, performing or speaking, which offered a way to step out of themselves and create a new experience for themselves.

Back in my shy days, acting was the very last thing that I wanted to do. However, my encounter with the nurse at RADA had lit a touch-paper in me and, at some level, I knew that drama was a pathway to becoming the person that I really wanted to be. That person is what I now call a sunflower – someone who always had this potential self locked away inside them and who, in the right atmosphere, can allow this potential self to blossom. That potential self lives inside you too. In the safe context of university, I was building my confidence every day and I was loving every minute of it. There was no big pressure on us to perform - it didn't matter whether we were good at drama or not. We were doing it for the fun of it and, as a result, it was fun. There was no one barking from the sidelines, telling us what we could or could not do, and making us feel self-conscious and exposed. We found our own way of doing what we wanted to do with support from our tutors, who were laid-back and having fun themselves. In that atmosphere any latent talent we had began to emerge, including mine.

In the expansive atmosphere of university, I was noticing how different I was feeling and behaving. I was speaking up in tutorials, speaking first rather than waiting for others to offer their opinions, and I found to my surprise that people were interested in what I had to say. The roles that I was playing on stage were giving me the means to behave in new ways, and performing in front of audiences was allowing me to feel more and more comfortable with exposure and being seen by others. I grew in confidence, which enabled me to further develop abilities that, only a few months before, I never knew I had.

It was all very surprising because I had struggled with English Literature and had done so little acting at school. Had this all been a reflection of how my teachers saw me and therefore how I saw myself because, as a wallflower, I was not expected to have an aptitude for drama? I firmly kept my light "under a bushel" and concealed it in the most shadowy parts of myself. I kept it hidden even from myself. This is true for many wallflowers. It had been so much easier for others to leave me on the sidelines, because it would have been much too much effort to help me to break out of my conditioning. This is the plight of many wallflowers who get pigeonholed in a certain way, and this sets up deep patterns that are hard to break later on in life.

Since my lecturers and fellow students saw me differently from that, without these preconceptions, it became safer for me to allow my true self to be seen - in particular the parts of myself I had learnt to keep hidden. My drama experiences were undoing all that old programming and I was building new foundations on which to construct my self-image. This was a totally new image, which bore little relation to the previous one. I was emerging from my shell and other students were seeing me as one of the confident ones. This is one of the key aspects of becoming a sunflower. Because other people were seeing me as confident, I began to see myself in that way. The positive atmosphere encountered at university had drawn out more of my natural abilities and I had blossomed. Although at first I had had to fake it a bit, the result of faking it had enabled genuine ability to emerge: the abilities that had been trapped inside me and never had a chance to grow. I have much evidence that this is true for most people. It's probably true for you too.

If, right now, you are freaking out at the thought of ever doing drama, just hang in there. Later on I will be explaining how the adapted drama I work with is designed for people who are self- conscious in the extreme, and who would never seek to participate in a normal drama class. If I hadn't had the positive experiences I have described, I would have stayed stuck on the sidelines and I would never have found this way forward.

## New challenges

When I went to university I had little idea of what I might do afterwards. I thought maybe of teaching but knew this was a safe option for me and I wasn't sure if it would take me forward.

Just at this point when I might have strayed off my path, Philip Roberts who had encouraged me throughout my drama journey, threw me a new challenge and suggested I pursue a career in acting. I was dumbstruck.

Much as I had thrived on all the acting I had done, I hadn't even dared dream that I could ever enter the profession, but Philip was firm in his conviction that this was the right path for me. I had such deep respect and admiration for Philip; I knew he wouldn't say anything he didn't mean. That night my brain was alive with thoughts. This was a new calling. I had no hope of ever being good enough to be a professional actress; my self-esteem was still fragile but I knew this path would take me forward.

Quite early on, I discovered the Actors Institute and participated in numerous courses and classes there. The Actors Institute was unusual in that it brought together personal development work and acting, and this was radical at the time, particularly within the acting profession. It was using drama as a way for people to free themselves to develop their potential. Whilst there, I was introduced to the work of Viola Spolin and Keith Johnstone (two important improvisation pioneers) through attending classes run by two gifted teachers, Andy Harmon and John Muirhead. I discovered that improvisation was nothing like I had thought it was. In auditions I had frozen every time I had been asked to improvise. The more assertive actor types had stolen the show, whilst the rest of us tagged along and felt rather lame. But I learned that this was not true improvisation.

Improvisation is not about initiating or being clever or showing off. Improvisation is about responding to others and following the natural flow of your impulses. Through these courses, I learned how to deeply connect with my instinctive self, to let go of my overactive mind and free myself of critical judgments (of myself and my abilities), so that I was free to follow the impulses that were naturally arising in me.

## Saying good-bye to social anxiety

In spite of the confidence I had built, I still found socialising difficult, particularly at larger gatherings, parties, or with people I didn't know. I found myself going blank, unable to think what to say. When someone cracked a joke, I never knew how to respond and I admired the people who were verbally fluent and could make others laugh.

But after doing a few improvisation courses, I found myself being able to do that too − and with ease. I was responding to witty remarks in a witty way and I was making people laugh. I had always had a good sense of humour − but only a very few people ever saw that. By applying the skills I had acquired through improvisation, this emerged naturally without me having to think about it, since these skills had become second nature.

My confidence in this area grew and I soon found parties and networking much easier. I could talk to anyone. I even at times found myself the life and soul of the party and the centre of attention, and I was surprised that, once again, it didn't feel so unnatural. Had I really been a wallflower all those years ago?

I began to use the same principles in other areas of my life. I started to go with the flow in my normal everyday life, and to trust more in my instincts − and I found that life had rather a wonderful way of unfolding. When I got stuck or encountered a problem, or things didn't work out quite the way I was expecting, I applied the same principles and found that soon a magical solution to the problem appeared without me having to do anything. I've been using this every since − and it has never yet failed me.

This has become the underpinning of the Sunflower Effect. I love seeing people who had originally classed themselves as wallflowers, discovering the same joy and freedom as I had. After that their lives can never be the same again.

## Setbacks

I would like to write that my pathway continued as it started bringing me success beyond my dreams. But from then on I still met many challenges and obstacles; there were *cul-de-sacs* along the way, along with moments when it felt I was making real headway. I learnt much about myself in the process. My struggles led me to personal growth work, and once more I took a leap forward. Gradually it was the personal growth work that brought me the kind of riches that I had originally experienced in acting.

I began on an inner journey. I learned many success tools, and discovered too that it was possible to achieve radical change if I put my mind to it, and this gave me hope that in time I could change many aspects of my experience. As a result, more and more of the sunflower in me began to emerge

Then I hit a major roadblock. I was offered the part to play the lead in a new play at the Edinburgh Festival. I was thrilled. My time at the Actors Institute had encouraged me to think big and to expand my horizons, and I was eager to take advantage of this opportunity. However, the rehearsal process was punishing and the director was using psychological techniques to bring out a very deep form of acting. He didn't realise that he was playing with fire. In a very traumatic exploratory improvisation I was taken into a very dark and terrifying place and I was faced with some of my deepest fears and insecurities, so when I played out the scene in the play, it was for real. The distinction between what was me and what was the character disappeared, and I was lost. Although the director did achieve his objective and those that saw the play were stunned by the raw emotion that was expressed - it was at a price. I was on the edge of a nervous breakdown. The play was seen by a very few people because the director had chosen a venue on the outskirts of the city and few ventured to see it; the play never even got to the starting post of attracting critical attention. All our hard work had been for nothing.

When I returned to London I was in a very bad way. Although I never had a breakdown I was deeply depressed, and my sunflower had seriously wilted. All the good work of the previous years had come to nothing. I was called for an audition for a prestigious regional theatre that had been keen to cast me earlier, but the director was disappointed with my audition and informed me I had lost my spark. It took me many years to recover from this. At university I had the opportunity to play a variety of roles, which enabled me to develop aspects of myself because the characters I was playing were nothing like me. Each part I had enabled me to explore aspects of myself but in the profession and particularly in this experience, I was being cast closer to myself and to my deepest wounds, which succeeded in drawing them out more. (I had discovered that, in the right hands, drama is deeply liberating - and, in the wrong hands, potentially damaging.) Whilst my determination to make a breakthrough kept me at it, by degrees I was losing my joy of performing.

## Becoming a writer

During my recovery period, I found myself at a writing workshop given by Tony Craze, who was then writer in residence at the Soho Poly Theatre (now the Soho Theatre). I had no illusions that I could ever be a writer; I just thought it sounded interesting. But it wasn't the normal kind of writing course. Tony got us to write scenes based on improvisations by actors. When my scene was read out, I was stunned and so was everyone else. There was something in the scene that could not be defined by the words on the page. Tony invited me to finish the play and gave me a date when my play would have a professional reading at the Soho Poly - a great honour.

Every morning I sat down to write. **Almost effortlessly I was accessing a very powerful place that enabled me to write the play like a dream.** This was the same place that I had accessed during the improvisation classes. Writing was really no different from improvisation. The play quite simply wrote itself.

When the play was read at the Soho Poly, it was clear that this was a very unusual script. Many years later, this play went on to become *Corryvreckan* and was produced at the Old Red Lion Theatre. It was shortlisted for Best Play; was nominated for three and won one award at the Fringe Theatre Awards; and two top literary agents wanted to represent me. Suddenly I found I was a playwright with an interesting and unique voice.

## Blessings in adversity

Although my near nervous breakdown had seemed like a disaster, and caused me immense suffering, it had brought many blessings. I would never have become a playwright if I hadn't had that experience, and I would have missed out on developing many different skills. My playwriting skills, on top of bringing me immense satisfaction and winning me accolades, had enabled me to develop other highly rewarding pieces of work.

Much later on I was asked by the Guildford School of Acting to devise a play for their post-graduate students. I used my playwriting skills to devise this play and I received the feedback that this had been the most successful devising project they had had at the drama school. I also used these skills when I was working for the Studio Upstairs, a mental health charity where I devised numerous riveting pieces of theatre with my performance group in a very short amount of time. But the biggest success for me was seeing members of my group, who were suffering from a wide range of mental health issues, including depression, schizophrenia and bi-polar disorder, exceed all expectations of what they could achieve – every one of them became a sunflower in the performance.

On top of all these positives, the near nervous breakdown was a time period of deep healing and questioning, and enabled me to delve more into my internal blocks and find a way though. All through this period I continued to invest in personal growth work, which continued to support and inspire me, enabling me to change my mindset, expand in new areas and work through these setbacks. This has enabled me to work with clients who feel as lost as I did: and for me to help them much faster and more effectively than I was through more traditional methods.

## Setting up Making Moves

Much later, it was through participating in a very challenging Leadership course that I began to take stock and review what was truly important to me. I realised that as much as acting had served to uncover my inner sunflower, if anything it was making me miserable. It had served its purpose. Though another synchronous set of circumstances, I found myself drawn to pursue a career in dramatherapy. Although I didn't really know what dramatherapy was, I just knew that this was a calling as powerful as when the night nurse had told me about her acting training. I was once more alive and with a direction to pursue, which I knew was the work I was meant to do and which brought together two important elements of my life - theatre and personal growth. Dramatherapy took me on a profound journey through which I learned how to work with drama safely. It was through this that I set up Making Moves, moving away from therapy and, over time, I evolved the Sunflower Effect, a personal development approach bringing together all that I had discovered in my own journey.

In the next chapter, we will be turning our attention back to you and your journey from wallflower to sunflower. You will be discovering how to avoid the pitfalls that keep many people stuck as wallflowers so that you can begin to make REAL progress.

## Chapter 5

# The Perks of Being a Wallflower

**The unique qualities of wallflowers that are often overlooked and how to change how you see yourself**

It is true; there is something about the sunflower that is hugely attractive both in nature and in life. It instantly grabs attention. In nature, the sunflower is set up to attract the sun. Its huge flower heads are suntraps and are rather like the sun itself. The French word for sunflower is "*tournesol*," which means "turns with the sun." This is a phenomenon when the sunflower is growing called heliotropism, due to the uneven distribution of a plant growth regulator, which causes the heads to be drawn towards the sun, and thus enables the head to absorb even more of the sun's powerful rays.

When someone walks into a garden, they are immediately drawn to the sunflower. This is the same for the sunflowers in life; other people are naturally attracted to the sunflower's radiant personality and everyone seems to gravitate to them - without the sunflower having to do anything, it seems

However, if the visitor to the garden moves across the lawn, they may find themselves inextricably drawn by a magnificent scent that is equally striking. They look around, not quite sure where it's coming from... that perfume which is the very essence of summer. What do they finally discover when they have hunted thoroughly around all the beds? None other than the common or garden wallflower is the source of this magnificent scent. Who would have thought it?

In fact the wallflower has something that the sunflower doesn't have: sunflowers have no perfume. Even magnificent roses, (except for a very few varieties) cannot rival the wallflower's scent, and most commercial roses have no scent at all.

## The unique qualities of wallflowers

So is it true that sunflowers have it all? In this respect, wallflowers are as attractive as sunflowers. It's just a different kind of attraction. In fact, wallflowers have very pretty flowers, if you actually look at them. It's just that they don't stand out. They are designed to blend in, but this doesn't take away from their beauty.

This is one of the positive aspects of being a wallflower: the ability to blend in. You have what author Robin Shohet calls the capacity to "combine" with others. This means you can easily be part of a group or team. You have an uncommon facility to adapt, to adjust yourself around others and this can be a very useful skill, particularly in situations where delicate negotiation is required. Since wallflowers dislike being the centre of attention, this means you don't stand out and gives certain advantages. Other people feel safe with you and they don't see you as a threat. Thus wallflowers excel as counselors, coaches, consultants, therapists, mediators, doctors and healers because of their capacity to sit and listen, and to facilitate change or healing in a person or organisation often without it appearing that they are doing anything.

These skills are uniquely the territory of wallflowers, but most wallflowers don't see it like that. As you saw in Chapter 3, if you have had people constantly telling you about all that you are lacking and what you need to do about it, then this sends a powerful message to your deeper self that you are "not OK." Then your own self-evaluation system begins to kick in, adding insult to injury. Soon this system, on its own, will be enough to keep you believing that, as a wallflower, you are seriously disadvantaged. It may be called the Critical Voice, the Inner Critic, the Chimp, the Negative Mind. Whatever it may be called, it's a powerful, self-inflicted undermining system that, in the long term, can give you a warped idea of your abilities.

This is part of your self-defence system, which I spoke about in the beginning of this book, where you are **literally fighting yourself.**

There is a saying: *"a city at war with itself cannot stand"*. One part of you is struggling to make some positive changes in your life and the other part is convinced this is impossible. This is very confusing and makes change very slow. Every time you make progress, this other part of you will undermine your best efforts and like two armies at war, where the small victories of one are soon reversed by the other, so neither can make any headway.

However, you can start to break out of this deadlock **by valuing the positive aspects of being a wallflower,** and seeing the hidden gift within aspects of your behaviour that you have previously seen as negative, or taken for granted.

## Wallflowers are happy being wallflowers

The truth is, in spite of all the negative connotations of being a wallflower discussed in this book so far, if you were an actual wallflower you would be very happy growing by your wall or in your clump because that is absolutely the best terrain for you. You would not be the only plant that loves walls. Lupins, foxgloves, honeysuckle and roses all love walls and no one thinks they are lesser for it.

Indeed, certain species of wallflowers have the capacity to grow in the most challenging terrains. Whilst I was planning this book my partner and I spotted a wallflower growing out of the cracks of a wall, a most inhospitable spot for any other flower, but there was the wallflower growing. You'll find the photo I took of this on the book's website.

So wallflowers are survivors. If you are a wallflower you are a survivor too. It was the wall that enabled you to survive, because without its protection you would have certainly shrivelled up and died. **You're still here.** You survived - even if you feel a bit like the wallflower I saw growing on the top of the wall.

It's time to acknowledge your achievement, even if you felt you had no other choice and you deemed that your survival was a monumental failure. As you will soon see, other people can often see qualities in the wallflower that they don't see - qualities that don't feel like advantages at all to the wallflower.

## What is a wallflower really?

So what is wallflower really? We may be familiar with the common dictionary definition: *A person who, because of shyness, unpopularity, or lack of a partner, remains at the side at a party or dance.*

However, this is far from the whole story. In some contexts the term wallflower is not just limited to individuals: it can also refer to groups and even organisations.

*Any person, organisation, etc., that remains on or has been forced to the sidelines of any activity*

Thus, an organisation may find themselves a wallflower, if due to swings in consumer behaviour, market forces or competition, they were forced into the sidelines. Just because they've moved to the sidelines doesn't mean that they're going to stay there. In fact their experience on the sidelines may be a valuable opportunity to develop new skills, discover new avenues, and may lead to opportunities that they would never have had if they weren't pushed out from their primary position. This could happen to a football team, an athlete, a billionaire – **it could happen to anyone.** Seen like this, the stigma of being a wallflower becomes much less.

You may be surprised to learn, how those who value the wallflower's positive qualities perceive wallflowers. Just a cursory exploration on the will bring up some surprising views on wallflowers, which I hope will enable you to see yourself and other wallflowers in a more positive light. The italics are mine.

- A type of loner. Seemingly shy folks *who no one really knows.* Often some of *the most interesting people,* if one actually talks to them.

- A person *who sees the world for what it really is*, all the beauty and the ugliness.

- Someone who knows life is only for the one *who is not afraid to die* and that joy is only for him - *who does not fear to be alone.*

- These are the most amazing people you will ever meet and *you will never, not even if you try, forget them.*

- A person who *sees everything and knows everything that's going on* - but doesn't say a word. They aren't loners - they are shy and don't choose to be in the mix of things.

- People nobody pays attention to and that fade into the background - but are really *genuine and interesting people if you take the time to get to know them.*

- Someone who chooses to observe, instead of experience, life. *They know a lot about people; what they are truthfully like; how they actually act when they think no one is paying attention.* Since people have little interest in wallflowers, they usually know a lot about people - the good and the bad.
- Wallflowers *are not mean, or impolite.* They are usually pleasant, and respectful - just shy and/or introverted.
- People who aren't necessarily shy, but never really tell you a lot about themselves. *They observe almost everything and listen to everything you have to say, without criticizing or judging.*
- These people are often *the most sincere, kind, and wonderfully interesting people* - yet fail to be attractive to the opposite sex for some reason.
- Someone who could be called shy; someone who doesn't feel comfortable around other people. *They don't like to have attention on them because it makes them uncomfortable.* They like to stay off to the side at parties or dances.
- They have trouble talking to people because *they don't know what to say.* Talking to new people is not their strongest point and *standing up in front of people can make them feel awful.*
- They may act fake around their friends to hide their real quiet personality, but to everyone else, they're invisible. Just because they're "antisocial" doesn't mean they're snobby. *They just would rather watch then be involved.*
- They know things about people that you would never know unless you watched as closely as them.

- *You could tell anything to a wallflower and they'd never tell anyone* because they try to avoid talking to people. They can be the best people - if you take the time to *crack their thick shell.*
- The opposite sex doesn't seem to consider them very much – but if you got to know them, they'd be great.
- They are usually attracted to other wallflowers because they are like each other. *Wallflowers are beautiful.*
- That wallflower is actually one of the most interesting people I've ever met.

*The Urban Dictionary*

These views are candid yet perceptive views of the wallflower's true nature - the truth that lies beneath what most wallflowers believe others perceive about them. We finally see wallflowers as they are: beautiful, vulnerable, kind and wise, along with many other wonderful qualities.

Do you see yourself in some of these comments? Do you find yourself focusing on the few negative aspects of the wallflower rather than the many positive qualities that are mentioned? Do you find yourself disbelieving these comments or that the writer really meant them? If you've received a lot of negativity from other people, this would not be surprising and, as you are probably aware, this is not going to help you move from wallflower to sunflower. In fact, it's going to keep you stuck as a wallflower, walking the wallflower treadmill, repeating the experiences that you long to put behind you.

## Changing how you see yourself

If you only see the wallflower as an outsider, a loser, a failure, a loner, weak, unpopular, with nothing to contribute, that's what the wallflower will become. However, this is only a reflection of your own fears and beliefs projected onto the wallflower. It's not who or what the wallflower really is. However if you start seeing the wallflower's real gifts, then suddenly you begin to see the wallflower in an entirely new light and open up a pathway for real change.

In psychology this is called **reframing your experience.** Because within your wallflower, hidden a long way beneath the surface, lies your potential to become a sunflower. Left untended, this potential will never emerge. However, if you nurture this potential within you, your inner sunflower will begin to sprout and take root. A very powerful way of doing this is by appreciating the positive aspects of being a wallflower. This is one of the ways of opening up your pathway from wallflower to sunflower.

This is one of the many paradoxes of the Sunflower Effect, that **in order to say goodbye to your wallflower identity, you need to embrace it fully.** It has been an essential part of you, and you can't just throw it away. Maybe in the process you will even start to like being a wallflower! This will hold you in good stead if ever your confidence is knocked and inevitably, you find yourself slipping back into feeling like a "negative" wallflower. This will help you to **reframe your experience** by embracing the true gift that it is to be a wallflower. Life is full of contrast. If it's good to be fully expressive, it's also good at other times to be reflective - to watch and observe. This will help you too to return faster to your naturally expressive self.

## The power of the observer

For many years I believed I was boring because I couldn't express what was within me. I didn't participate much unless the conditions were right. My place was to watch and to keep quiet. Yet we have just seen the repeated admiration for the wallflower's capacity to observe because *"no one else is watching that closely."*

The wallflower's preference for the sidelines means they are in an ideal position to stand back and see the truth that no one else can see. However, because they can be so focused on their own self- consciousness and are fearful that they won't be heard or understood if they expressed what they see, the wallflower keeps silent, often believing that their perspective is obvious to everyone, or that others will misunderstand them.

Even highly intelligent and gifted people do this because they don't appreciate how valuable their contribution is and, as a result, they deprive others and often the world of their unique perspective. Wallflowers keep quiet because, even though they know deep within themselves that they need to speak up, **they simply can't**. And this inability to speak often leaves them with a deep sense of unworthiness, failure, shame and isolation from other people.

This ability to stand back and observe is just one of the many skills that you may have developed in your time on the sidelines. I have been struck on so many occasions by the contribution that quieter, deeply thinking people can make in the right environment. I am surprised by the depth of their understanding or the freshness with which they perceive a situation, or their capacity to delve below the surface and to express themselves in a way that is unique to them. This is often the kind of person who is so reserved that most people don't even notice them and wouldn't even think to seek out their opinion. The person doesn't see what they have expressed as anything unusual because it's just what is going on in their own head.

## Sally

*Sally was a consultant. She'd risen to this position because she was very good on paper and in one-to-one situations - but she was unable* to speak up in meetings when important ideas were discussed. Even though she had plenty of ideas she never said a word, except when she was directly asked a question, so her colleagues assumed she didn't have any ideas. It soon became clear, after Sally had done some powerful work in the Breakthrough Group, that her quiet manner carried a powerful authority and she had a way of conveying information that made everyone listen. Sally had no idea she had these qualities.

**KEY POINT: start valuing your thoughts and gut feelings**

Do you do this too? Even if you're not quite ready to speak up, I invite you to value this aspect of yourself: the thoughts you have whilst you listen, the ideas that wake you in the night, your ability to see the deeper truth in an individual or idea, or to know instinctively when someone is hiding the truth.

Your presence on the sidelines means that you are often there when others are too preoccupied with other matters, so you see the very thing that everyone else is missing. Take a moment to absorb just how valuable this ability is and what a great quality it is. Perhaps the next time you are in the same position as Sally was, you can remind yourself of the valuable contribution that you could be making. And if it feels important take a risk and speak up. Do this without any expectation that others will hear you or value what you are saying. As you grow in confidence, your words will carry more weight and others will listen to you. You may need some help in communicating your message with confidence and authority. Seek out that help. You will find some guidance about this at the end of this book.

## The perks of being a wallflower

When Steven Chobsky was at college, instead of being out with everyone else having a good time, he found himself choosing to work on one of his creative projects. Actually working on the project was a lot more enjoyable for him than being out with the crowd. He even found himself saying to himself: *"This has to be one of the perks of being a wallflower"* and he realised, even as he said this, that he had a very good title for a book - a book that he later went on to write and eventually have made into a highly rated film.

Whilst you are being a wallflower, you are not wasting your life away on the sidelines, even if it feels like it. A powerful process is going on. You are developing skills and resources that are going to bring you huge perks when you move from wallflower to sunflower. Even your most destructive experiences can have a "silver lining," a benefit: it's just a question of seeking out the silver lining and finding another way of viewing your experiences.

## Some of my perks

In my days as a wallflower, retreating into my internal world felt like my only option, since the world around me often felt unsafe. In my internal world, I was protected and no one could get at me (other than myself). I became an avid reader. I loved books. When I was reading a book I could escape from reality and enter completely into the world of the novel or story. Often the world I created inside my head was more real than the outside world. Certainly I preferred it because I could control it. If I didn't like what was happening in the story, I could stop reading and read another story. Or, I could wait until I felt ready to read that bit of the story.

Maybe the character was going through similar experiences to me and, when I returned to the story, I would learn a different way of coping with a situation, which I was not able to do in my real life. If the character was more expressive than I was, more able to speak up for themselves, I could vicariously piggy-back on their experience and pretend it was me. Therefore reading books was also enabling me to process my experiences and feel better about myself. Through this, I was developing my imagination, which has become a powerful resource for change and also an area of deep personal fulfilment in my life. I now teach other people how to use their imagination to change their life in this way.

Through reading books I was learning about life, and this rapidly turned me into a student of life. Because I was overwhelmed and perplexed about some of the experiences in my life, I was intent in understanding more about life and what made both me and other people tick. This has turned into a lifelong quest for learning. For a while this was academic learning but rapidly this turned into a fascination with personal development, and other forms of self- improvement.

I became, and continue to be, fascinated with stories as a learning tool. This is one of the key components of the Sunflower Effect. I am still an avid reader and student of life. I never stop learning and I don't think I ever will. Over time I discovered my internal world is a powerful resource that has been an absolute life-saver at different times in my life. It's the place that I now consciously go to when I am facing challenges. Later on in this book, you will have an opportunity to participate in a powerful process that will enable you to do the same. My internal world is much more than that. I need it like I need food and nurture. If I go without it for too long, I become anxious and stressed. It's where I also do my most powerful thinking and processing. Sometimes I just take myself to bed to allow myself to be able to receive its benefits. In the warmth of my bed I can recharge my batteries if they have become depleted. If you are an introvert you will need to do the same thing – although you may find a different way of achieving this. I now teach my clients to do this. Instead of criticising themselves for retreating into their shell, they realise it can be a positive place so long as they don't stay there too long.

Even being too good had its perks. In my school days I had constantly been awarded the politeness and kindness badge, even though I would have much preferred to be awarded more academic badges. However, I am not surprised I was awarded those badges in preference to other children because kindness and politeness have become second nature. It was an **adaptive pattern** (see Eric Berne's book *Games People Play: The Psychology of Human Relationships,*) and a strategy I had developed to survive the early experiences of my life - not very healthy, but it can still be a positive resource.

Being kind meant it was very easy for me to be compassionate to others and in time to learn to be compassionate to myself. It has helped me in the work I have chosen to do, which has enabled me to facilitate the several thousand people who have attended my courses to make powerful changes in their lives. Being polite has oiled the wheels of many difficult relationships that I have encountered in my life. My politeness has enabled me to deliver a difficult message in a way that is easier for other people to receive. I had to eradicate over- politeness and inauthentic politeness that were part of my adaptive conditioning. Being kind and polite means that I excel on the art of getting along with other people. Therefore I find it easy to get along even with very challenging people that other people avoid or fear.

Even my adaptive conditioning has had its benefits. I learned how to adapt myself around other people, and this has in the long term enabled me to easily adapt to new situations; to make the best of a difficult situation; and just to keep going when others would give up by finding a loop-hole or a way round an obstacle that was not so obvious to others. This also gave me the ability to pick up the unspoken, unconscious messages that other people are communicating, and this has enabled me to help them shift at a deeper level. This means that even when people are reacting or behaving in a negative way, I can see what lies behind their behavior - the pain and the vulnerability they are unconsciously trying to protect. I can hear the message that lies beneath their words and respond in a compassionate way.

In time, I discovered that being on the sidelines could be an equally positive place. I was learning through observing how others were "winning friends and influencing people". Even though I didn't have the skill or the nerve to do what they were doing - because I feared I would fall flat on my face, however I stored it all away. So when I did eventually acquire the confidence to express myself in this way, as a result of my drama experiences – this easy way of relating to others came naturally to me.

But the most positive aspect of all this is in the way I work from the sidelines. I realised early on in my work that I didn't operate at my best if I was leading from the front of a group, as is the traditional facilitator/leader role. The kind of process I have developed involves me stepping back at regular intervals. Then my participants have a chance to explore on their own and express themselves more freely. One of the nicest things that one of my clients wrote about me, many years ago, that has stuck with me, is:

*"What I really like about the way you work is that often you're just sitting in corner and letting us get on with it. It appears as if you're doing nothing, but I feel that at the same time you are putting your arms around the whole group so we can find our own capacity to shine."*

This feedback enabled me to transform my negative judgment of my capabilities. I was not like other workshop leaders, true, but my style of leading was indeed a lot more effective in empowering the clients that were attracted to my work. It was why I have been so successful in helping these people.

Much later in life when I had reached a dead end, where it felt like there were difficulties every way I turned and I was getting nowhere fast, a coach I was working with, Danusia Malina-Derben, pointed out a very obvious thing. The thing that I most wanted to hide from other people - my being a wallflower, my shyness, my low self-esteem, my years being too terrified to speak up and being taken advantage by other people - was in fact my greatest gift. It was a significant thing that I had got over these difficulties and put them behind me. I could help people who felt like me, do the same.

This is what I've been doing ever since and it was how that I came to develop the Sunflower Effect and write this book. It took me some time to create all this, as I have always been a slow learner and the process has needed time to evolve. The more I walked this path, the happier I felt. Every time I saw someone take the first, small step to liberate themselves, my heart leapt. I remembered back to the time when I felt so lost and helpless, and the miracle of setting myself free. Almost every experience I have had in my life, including my most destructive experiences, have become a means for helping others through understanding myself and other wallflowers better.

**Exercise: What are your perks?**

So now it's over to you. What are your perks of being a wallflower? Have you developed a talent or discovered a hidden ability or dream as a result of being a wallflower– even if you don't feel ready to share it with others quite yet? What are you good at? What do you most enjoy doing? Can you find a potential positive in this thing? Are you a good friend, a good listener, a great organiser? Do you have a knack of doing a task, or fixing a problem?

Some of these abilities may come as a result of being a wallflower and others may be just talents you have. It may be your ability to endure a very painful childhood, or to survive a life-threatening illness or a mental health condition. You are indeed a hero if you got through any of these things.

Write them down in your notebook, and leave plenty of space so you can add to them as ideas occur to you.

If you did the Powerful Decisions exercise, take a look at some of the experiences you've jotted down and the decisions you made that eventually became limiting beliefs. See now if you can find the "silver lining" in your wallflower experience. Write these down too.

If you're at the beginning of your journey, you may not have the kind of overview that I have because I've been at this game a lot longer. But see if you can find the seed of something that has developed in you, however small it might seem to you. It will develop in time, if you give it a chance, and the more you allow it to flower without judging, the more likely it will develop into something significant and meaningful for you. You may in time discover the inspiration for a career that will fulfil you far beyond your wildest dreams. If you find yourself feeling stuck you can express your perks as a hope or a dream. There's no knowing what might unfold over time.

Return to your list on a regular basis and review your list. Notice how you feel as you read it through. If you feel awkward or embarrassed or silly, this is to be expected if you're not used to doing this kind of exercise. This exercise is one of the building blocks of confidence, and is one of the simplest tools for building a lasting confidence. You will be expanding this in the next exercise in this chapter.

## Wallflowers don't see sunflowers clearly

In spite of the wallflower's sophisticated powers of observation, the one area where wallflowers don't see clearly is concerning sunflowers. This is because you are too close to feeling the pain of the wallflower. In other words, wallflowers are not very good at observing themselves.

You may be surprised to learn that many of the people that you perceive as sunflowers actually used to be wallflowers. They used to be just like you – **and if they can do it, so can you.** In fact what you admire in sunflowers are often the very qualities that are within you and are ripe for being developed in you, but you just don't see this. There is, in fact, an inner radiance within you that you have kept so hidden that it's barely visible. This is because most wallflowers have a warped view of what a sunflower really is.

When I was researching sunflowers for this book I was surprised how very accurate the botanical sunflower was as a symbol for what a human wallflower could become. Sunflowers in nature are not just stunning to look at it. They are hardworking plants, not just garden flowers. They have been cultivated and grown for at least 4500 years for their seeds and since the 1700's, to make sunflower oil. It's common to see thousands of sunflowers grown in a field.

Human sunflowers, like wallflowers, are great team players. They operate in groups and their true beauty lies in their ability to be part of something bigger; not to seek personal aggrandisement; not to aspire to be better than anyone else - but to share themselves with everyone. The human wallflower often can't see beyond the potential threat that the sunflower poses for them. All they can see is their own judgment of themselves and all the ways they are lacking, in comparison to the sunflower.

Indeed, the botanical sunflower is not just attractive. It's so much more than that.

- The Sunflower head is not the actual flower. It's actually a receptacle base of 1,000 to 2,000 tiny individual flowers.
- The Sunflower is not just an attractive garden flower; it's also an agricultural worker. The tiny flowers produce the seeds, which are highly nutritious, containing calcium and 11 other important minerals, and are becoming increasing popular for healthy snacking. The oil that is extracted from the seeds is widely used in culinary practice.
- Reducing heart disease: there are many products that are made from sunflower oil, since it's a good fat, helping to reduce heart disease.
- Ancient therapeutic benefits: it's believed that many ancient cultures used the sunflower for its therapeutic properties to treat skin conditions, sinusitis, haemorrhoids and leg ulcers.
- Removing toxins from the environment: sunflowers are used to extract toxins such as lead, arsenic and uranium from contaminated soil. They were used to remove toxins after the Chernobyl nuclear disaster and the Fukushima disaster.

It's not surprising that wallflowers don't see sunflowers clearly. We are brought up in a competitive world where there are winners and losers: so that when someone else is successful it means that you will fail. Thus, if the sunflower is shining, then the wallflower can't shine too.

## We are all meant to shine

You may be familiar with Marianne Williamson's famous words:

*"Your playing small does not serve the world. There is nothing enlightened about shrinking so that other people won't feel insecure around you. We are all meant to shine, as children do."*

**Marianne Williamson**, *A Return to Love*

The Aztec and the Inca cultures believed that the sunflower represented the sun and therefore worshipped it accordingly – because for them the sun represented the source of life itself. The sunflower's symbolism puts out a powerful message. We are all radiant; we all have that potential to shine; we all have amazing qualities within us that often are undiscovered or misunderstood. It's our birthright to develop these qualities, to develop our potential and to share this with others so that:

*"...as we let our own light shine, we unconsciously give other people permission to do the same. As we are liberated from our own fear, our presence automatically liberates others."*

**Marianne Williamson**, *A Return to Love*

It's not a selfish thing. It's not "Look at me, aren't I great?" and it's a far cry from the chant, "I'm the king of the castle." In fact the opposite is true. When you shine, it encourages others to shine too. I've seen this over and over again with my clients. When one person steps out of their comfort zone and liberates themselves, everyone else feels it's safe to do so too.

This is because it's a bold thing to step beyond what is familiar and to meet your own uncertainty, your vulnerability, in which you fear you won't know what to do. However, it is in that very "not knowing" that your freedom lies. If you always know what to do then you are bound. You are like an animal on a treadmill, just repeating the same pattern over and over again. But when you move into the area of **not knowing,** you free yourself - and when you do this anything can happen.

A wallflower will think that the worst will happen if they step out of their comfort zone, because that has been their experience, and they are stuck on that treadmill and locked into their fear. They feel they have no other choice than to keep repeating the pattern that reinforces their mistaken belief about themselves. However, when they step beyond those bounds, they step into whole new possibilities for themselves: possibilities that will open up a whole new world for them. This is the path of this book.

**Exercise: Let yourself shine**

**Step 1** Close your eyes and run through all your perks, your qualities, the things other people say about you, or some of the qualities that have been listed in this chapter that relate to you. Take a moment to appreciate these qualities one by one. See each quality as part of your own inner sunflower.

**Step 2** Imagine the warmth of the sun shining on each quality so it can begin to shine from the inside (it may not be very bright yet). Let yourself shine and bask in your own shining light. Take as long as you need to really feel your own shining light - so you can anchor this experience.

**Step 3** Afterwards, in your notebook list the feelings you noticed as you experienced your own shining light. Add any extra qualities that occurred to you during the exercise. You can add to them any time. Do this regularly so can begin to believe in your own shining light and your potential to become a sunflower.

**NOTE:** One of the most powerful ways of changing how you see yourself, as mentioned before, is changing the beliefs that you have acquired as a result of your adaptive conditioning. Many of the exercises in this book will address this, and help you to change these undermining beliefs, particularly the bonus exercise in Chapter 3.

## The power of joining with others

The wallflower's default mode is to operate alone and to feel apart from others but, the deeper your disconnection the more you will feel separate and apart. However, when you begin to join with others, particularly with other wallflowers, in a context where there is honest communication and you won't need to hide your vulnerabilities, then you can begin to see that others share your experiences. It's a human experience, not a failing or something to be kept hidden, **and might even have certain advantages.**

This is why I believe that true freedom for wallflowers happens in groups. This is why I work with groups; and it's in groups that my clients make the biggest shifts. In nature, the wallflower has a natural affinity to being part of a group since wallflowers are grown in clumps or swathes, so that together their outstanding perfume can make a real impact. This may not be easy for you right now and being in a group may be your worst nightmare; and it's important that you find a way to participate in a way that is positive for you. At the time of writing I am seeking out ways for you to connect with other people who share your wallflower experience. So if you signed up for the book's bonuses, I will be telling you about that when it's available.

## Sunflowers have a lot in common with wallflowers

Indeed, wallflowers have a lot more in common with sunflowers than they know. They are both great team players but in different ways. Sunflowers are very comfortable in groups. It's through being in a group that more of their true nature can shine, because shining is natural to sunflowers. They can't help it; it's part of their nature. It is their job.

The sunflower knows that the energy of the sun is infinite; it shines on everything equally. In time as the sunflower part of you begins to expand. You may find, like me, that you even thrive and enjoy being in larger groups. I remember how threatened and self-conscious I felt. But this very soon became a thing of the past, and it's now only in very extreme circumstances that I find myself reverting back to that old place - and I'm able to move myself out of that place pretty quickly.

In the next chapter I will be explaining how the Sunflower Effect works and the factors that enabled me to make such a dramatic shift from wallflower to sunflower. You will learn too, what makes it so different from other confidence and assertiveness techniques.

## Chapter 6

# The Sunflower Effect

**The Missing Link that will move you from wallflower to sunflower - even if you have zero self-belief and low expectations of what you can achieve**

The Sunflower Effect is a process. It's not a list of components that can be separated out. The Sunflower Effect is the result of all its elements working together as one, weaving together in different combinations in the same way as a flock of starlings fly together, moving together as one whilst creating a whole array of wonderful formations in the sky as they swoop and dive. They are constantly adjusting to each other, changing positions. Sometimes one is leading, sometimes another. How do they do that? It's a kind of magic.

This is how the Sunflower Effect works. It doesn't matter if you have more of one element than another or even that certain elements are missing; the Sunflower Effect still will be effective for you. All that the Sunflower Effect requires is that you show up and "be present." It doesn't matter if you are terrified, don't believe that you can do it, fear you might make a mistake or make a fool of yourself. You cannot fail, because every failure leads to success. It's not about **doing**; it's about **being**. When you are being a sunflower, you don't have to do anything. **It's who you are.**

Shortly, I will be asking you to imagine each letter of the word S U N F L O W E R as a means to take you across the fast-moving River of Life to where the sunflowers live. It doesn't matter if you don't yet believe you can get across the river; all you have to do is to get started. Only when you have reached the other side of the river will you know that you have arrived. Usually this happens at the end of one of my courses, when you look back at the person you were when you started the course and the person you have become; the confidence you have gained; and the whole raft of things you can do with ease that you couldn't before. But even if you are not able to attend one of my courses, I hope that the information in this chapter and the exercises towards the end of the book will inspire you to find your own way of achieving a profound shift in your confidence level.

Confidence is not a static thing; it's constantly in motion; it also has a tendency to go up and down. When you lose confidence, it can be hard to get it back. However, as you meet challenges in your life and overcome them, your confidence will mature and eventually you will easily overcome the things that used to knock you sideways. As long as you keep putting the Sunflower Effect into practice your confidence will continue to grow. When you do this, opportunities will come your way without your even seeking them out. You will live your life in flow, and discover what fulfils you at the deepest level.

## Bonus 3

See Bonus 3, *The Self Confidence Myth,* a 50 page e-book which complements the ideas expressed in this book, particularly this chapter and will support you on your journey from wallflower to sunflower. If others have told you that you lack confidence, the book demonstrates that it's a **myth that you lack confidence.** If you haven't yet downloaded the bonuses, you can download this along with my other bonuses by visiting fromwallflowertosunflower.com.

## The nine elements of the Sunflower Effect

    S  for Safety

    U  for Unconscious blocks

    N  for Natural

    F  for Freedom

    L  for Letting go

    O  for Out of your head

    W  for Witnessing

    E  for Expression

    R  for Repetition

    S  is for safety

**Safety** is really important if you have retreated into your shell. This is one of the primary reasons why you feel like a wallflower. You retreated into your shell because it felt safe there. However, when it comes to coming out of your shell, you absolutely need a safe place in order to emerge fully from your place of retreat, or you'll find yourself back there only too soon – as you know only too well.

One of the most important components of the Sunflower Effect is providing that safe space. This is what I provide through my courses. It's important that this is a **non-judgmental space**. It's criticism that killed your confidence - parents, teachers, bosses, managers are mistaken in thinking that if they criticise you, they are helping you to learn. In fact, what they are doing is making you afraid of making a mistake and of failing. Through this they are also creating a destructive psychological mechanism that is going to block your progress. Thus, instead of them criticising you, you begin to criticise yourself.

Indeed, many of my clients discover that their head is so full of critical thoughts that they are unable to think straight. This is particularly true in a situation where they feel under pressure; where there is an expectation for them to perform; where they feel others are judging them; if they've been teased or laughed at; or where they're afraid of making a mistake because they've made a mess on a previous occasion.

Having a non-judgmental space releases you from these pressures and gives you permission to make mistakes. (Actually it's quite hard to make mistakes when you're trying to do it deliberately). This is particularly important if you've been made to feel that you should be different from the way you are or if you have had to conform to the expectations of others. This is why, too, every activity in my courses is an invitation, an opportunity to stretch or to take a risk and do something you don't usually do. You can apply this to any activity in your life where you have a chance to move out of your comfort zone. Instead of pressuring yourself to do it; invite yourself into the experience with no expectations that you will achieve anything.

Knowing that it's your choice to take that step immediately gives you power and frees you to find your true, authentic expression. Try it.

## U is for unconscious blocks

Sunflowers have self-belief. It's very difficult to express yourself in this way when you are sitting on a lot of repressed, unconscious emotion. This is deep emotion that lies beneath the surface. This is often connected to a painful experience which you had in the past that you thought you had fixed, or that you wish you didn't have to deal with. It's hard to truly move from wallflower to sunflower without removing the destructive effects of this unconscious programming. Unconscious blocks keep us repeating the same habitual patterns over and over again.

One of the most powerful aspects of the Sunflower Effect is its capacity to transform these **unconscious blocks** as I will explain later. The Resistor is part of your self-defence system that resists change and lives in you at an unconscious level. This is what makes it so hard to change - because the Resistor is very skilled at resisting and evading detection.

You need to reach it at the unconscious level. However, it's not easy to work with the unconscious through the analytical mind - through talking about it – because the unconscious does not operate through words. This is why most talking therapies can only go so far. We have to reach the unconscious in a language it understands. This is why the Sunflower Effect is so effective, since it works in a language that the unconscious does understand - through symbol, metaphor and story.

Unconscious learning goes very deep. So when you start learning at an unconscious level, which is how we are going to work later in this book, it will enable you to progress much faster and it will also enable you to keep on shifting, and dissolving ever-deeper levels of resistance and stuckness. Once you have reached those deeper levels of resistance you will start making significant shifts. This is why radical transformation can be achieved through the Sunflower Effect. I explain more about this in the next chapter.

## N is for natural

Sunflowers are **naturally** confident. In truth, everyone has that inner confidence that lives inside them. If you doubt that it's there, it's just that you have yet to discover it.

Confidence is not worth anything unless it feels natural. It's not enough to learn a confidence technique, or to discover a way of communicating that achieves results. Confidence needs to come from that natural place in you or it will appear fake, and over time you just won't be comfortable expressing yourself in that way. This is what will make it **second nature,** and this is what the Sunflower Effect will develop in you over time. In my courses you can learn how to access this natural place so it feels that your confident behaviour is genuinely coming from you. You will also get a taste of how to access this through the exercises later on in this book.

This is what Eric Berne calls the **natural child.** Every adapted child can become a natural child through the Sunflower Effect. It's about unlearning your adapted behaviours so you can recover your natural and authentic responses.

## F is for freedom

Most wallflowers don't feel free. They feel as if they are in a box, constricted and inhibited. If you find yourself in this paralysed place that is run by your **fear**, then, even though you may deeply want to be free of this, you are aware that there is something deep inside that is blocking you. The Sunflower Effect will enable you to discover the freedom to liberate yourself so that you can express yourself **without** fear. Until you discover that freedom within you, it will be very hard for you to be a sunflower and be confident in the way that you want to.

The Sunflower Effect uses an especially adapted form of drama (based in dramatherapy), designed for people with no experiences or aptitude for drama. Working with this kind of drama is the easiest way of accessing this freedom. Drama physically releases you – that is, you **have to** release and thus free yourself when you do drama. This works in connection with Safety. The drama exercises that you will do in the

Sunflower Effect will enable you to experience your fear in a very safe environment so you can move through your fear, and in time liberate it and transform it into excitement, which will carry you into new expression. This is what makes the difference between having a traumatic experience that you never want to repeat as described in Chapter 2, and having an experience that is going to free you to be your true self.

The Sunflower Effect offers an opportunity to stand outside yourself; to leave your familiar self behind; to step into another character; and behave the way that character behaves without any of the associations that you have with your own behaviour. This is another kind of freedom. In fact, it's your habitual forms of behaviour and the way in which you seek approval from others that is keeping you so constricted. When you free yourself from these behaviours through playing a dramatic character, you start breaking those old patterns.

Through this, you are also expanding your comfort zone. When you move out of your comfort zone, you stretch your comfort zone just a bit more, so you are occupying a bigger space. As you become accustomed to this bigger space, in time you will begin expressing yourself in a way that fits this larger space. As you become comfortable in this bigger space you will be ready to expand even more - you will become more empowered, **more free** each time you expand.

At a certain point as you continue to expand, you may find your fear levels increasing. But this is natural. It's important to take your time and get the support you need to move through your fear, so you can continue to expand. Every time someone steps out of their comfort zone and liberates themselves, it liberates everyone and gives them the permission to set themselves free too. This is why it's so powerful to do this within a group.

When you start finding that freedom to express yourself in this way, you will be amazed at the difference it makes in your communication and your ability to respond to what's happening around you. You are opening yourself up in all sorts of ways and awakening the dormant parts of yourself that have been locked away - maybe for a very long time. This is going to make you appear more open and approachable to other people, which is one of the building blocks of social confidence.

## L is for letting go

If you have been through a lot of negative experiences connected to being a wallflower, you will have a lot of stored memories (both conscious and unconscious) that are constantly being triggered as you encounter similar experiences. As that old memory is stimulated, you will find yourself automatically playing out the same adaptive behaviour, which is connected to old behaviour patterns and beliefs that are no longer serving you. So these are all the things that you need to let go of if you're going to change your *modus operandi*. In computer terms, you need to put the old memories, beliefs and patterns in the trash bin, and then **empty the trash bin.** This will change the energy that you are carrying and, in effect, will close down the "programs" that you no longer need so you can be in an **open** place to create new programs.

This is a complex process. It's actually really difficult to let go of emotional content; particularly content that has an unconscious element, for the reasons I've previously described. You may find yourself unwilling to empty the trash bin, since there's a complex psychological process that keeps us attached to your old patterns, just in the same way as you may be unwilling to throw things away in case you might need them one day. The Sunflower Effect will enable you to release and let go of these old patterns bit by bit, even the ones that are deeply hard-wired, by working through unconscious blocks and freeing yourself from their power over you. It will also automatically change the brain-wave patterns that are creating stress and fatigue, which will assist with the letting go process. Research into brave-wave patterns shows there are certain brain-wave patterns that enable us to function more effectively - an imbalance thus will foster anxiety, depression, stress etc. The Sunflower Effect is also effective at helping you to release these disempowering states.

The Sunflower Effect works through play and though having fun, and this is incredibly important in the letting go process because it distracts the Resistor. When you are enjoying yourself, the Resistor believes there is "nothing serious going on" and so it relaxes. This will allow the deeper work to go on without any interference, enabling you to free the emotions that have been buried at an unconscious level, and to **let go** of the repressed traumatic experiences that you have been carrying. Mostly you won't know it's happening because your conscious mind believes that you are playing and having fun - although you may feel something shifting inside you, feel heavier than usual after the session or start dreaming a lot. One of my clients has named this kind of play Profound Play. It's one of the unique aspects of the Sunflower Effect that enables you to let go of this programming faster than most other methods.

## O is for out of your head

Being in your head blocks you from accessing your intuitive side and your natural wisdom. It keeps you in compulsive thinking, analysing and anxiety that keeps you in your analytical mind. These states stimulate the **limbic system** of the brain, which activates fear and keeps adrenaline pumping round your body. This is a vicious circle that keeps you going round and round on a treadmill of old thought patterns and destructive emotions. The Sunflower Effect breaks this vicious circle, moves you out of your head and into the present moment. It teaches you how to operate through your whole brain – so that your analytic and intuitive faculties work in harmony together. When one part of your habitual mindset shifts, all others automatically begin to shift. This is multi-dimensional process (not a linear process) which is what leads to **the whole mindset changing** and, eventually, to lasting confidence. With your new mindset, you will almost inevitably start creating more successful experiences so that you are more often "getting it right". This is where all those people who criticised you come into play. If just one of them starts to acknowledge you or praise you or to grudgingly give you a more positive performance review (because this is the kind of person they are), then this will make an incredible difference to you (see Witnessing). You will feel you really are making headway.

As a result of living more out of your head and more in your natural flow, you will begin to create an **incredible amount of ease in your life.** Things will just somehow work out for you. Opportunities will come your way that seem to come from nowhere. You won't know where that opportunity came from; it just arrived out of the blue. After a while you won't have to get anxious about things not working out, because you will have built up a trust in knowing that everything will work out. You will build a trust in this momentum and start living your life in flow, as a river flows without fearing that its source will dry up. This is a very natural way of living your life.

One of the most powerful and transformational things you can do is **stop being afraid of getting it wrong.** Through giving yourself permission to make mistakes in a safe environment, you will automatically move out of your head and into your intuitive capacity. You will free yourself to be truly yourself – the self that you are truly are, the self that you were before you withdrew into your shell. You will find yourself experiencing true freedom. At first it will be little glimpses, but gradually these will increase until you find there are whole tracts of time when you are living out of your head and in tune with your natural impulses.

## W is for witnessing

Witnessing is unique to the Sunflower Effect and is one of the reasons why it achieves such significant shifts in a relatively short amount of time. Witnessing is about **being seen.** Wallflowers are anxious about being seen because their expectation is that they will be seen in a critical or negative light. Witnessing in a safe, supportive and compassionate environment will enable you to transform the negative effects of these experiences. When other people witness the changes you are making, it feels more real. It's real because other people saw and acknowledged what had happened. A witness is one who not only sees but also **testifies** and therefore their words can carry immense weight.

In the Sunflower Effect the witnesses are **empathic witnesses:** those that witness with compassion, empathy and kindness. The witnesses offer positive reflections of what they are seeing you express and, through this process, you will learn how to receive praise and acknowledgement from other people for what you are achieving and for the strengths they see in you. As you allow yourself to let this in, you will begin to open up to a different way of seeing yourself. This aspect on its own will build self-esteem, change your mindset and open up new possibilities for yourself also. Also it's as powerful to witness as to be witnessed, since, in witnessing another person you free yourself through empowering them. You will learn, through this process of witnessing how to become an empathic witness for yourself as well as other people.

This is achieved through the "mirror effect," a recognised psychological process. What you see in another is also in yourself (at some level); otherwise, you couldn't see it. As you acknowledge another you also acknowledge yourself, and this allows you to see hidden aspects of yourself so they, too, can grow. This will also assist to build greater self-esteem over time, if you can let it in. (This is often not easy for wallflowers because they have received such intensive negative programming that they will find themselves pushing away, denying or disbelieving the positive input they are receiving from others. Through practicing letting in positive reflections, this will gradually dissolve.)

It's even more powerful when you are witnessed releasing an unconscious block though the Sunflower Effect. This kind of witnessing, in effect, magnifies the release and letting go of the block. Something magical seems to happen when this takes place. Participants describe this in various ways: feeling a tingling at the back of the neck; as if a weight has been lifted off their shoulders; feeling light headed; feeling as if something has happened but they don't know what; or feeling immensely happy. It's as if the energy exchange between them and the empathic witnesses has brought about a fundamental shift. After such experiences, participants commonly report inexplicable shifts in their outside life. Speaking up in situations they would normally keep quiet; being more visible; feeling lighter; depression lifting, old habits that simply slip away etc.

When you are witnessed expressing your sunflower, in however small a way, those who witness you become part of your new audience who are cheering you and celebrating with you, as you achieve even greater success. This is the power of witnessing, and this is why being witnessed in the way I have described is going to gradually change your mindset. Empathic witnesses are on your side and they are saying "yes" to you every step of the way. They are mentors, celebrating with you when you succeed. They are holding your hand when you have a setback; pointing out all the things that worked; supporting you in understanding that in time you will put this behind you and achieve even greater success. With this kind of support almost, anything can be achieved.

If you are not able to participate in a group, then you will need to use imaginative means. See the commitment video in Bonus 1 and the tools and resources in the last chapter of this book.

## E is for expression

**Empowering expression** is what sunflowers do. They communicate in ways in which they are heard and this makes a difference to how they are seen by others. Wallflowers rarely express themselves in this way and, if they do, they are not heard, or continue to be ignored and discounted. What is going to enable you to end your time as a wallflower is having the freedom to express yourself and to release the impact of some of the negative experiences that have undermined your confidence.

This is what people experience on my courses in a context and an environment where empowering and transformational expression can take place. This is the kind of expression that is going to bring about change to your mindset and how you experience yourself on a day- to-day basis. This kind of expression is what is going to produce the energy and expansion that is needed to keep going and to keep expanding at ever-deeper levels.

One of the things that you will learn through the Sunflower Effect is to connect with your solar plexus, because that is where the core part of your self lives. This is the "sunflower" that you carry around with you: the sol or sun that lives in the centre of your body (your solar plexus). Actors call this part of themselves their "centre" and in the Indian chakra system this is coloured yellow and represented symbolically as the "sun". When you express from this place, it leads to authentic expression: the expression that sunflowers naturally do without needing think about it.

You will achieve authentic expression too, when you release emotional baggage that is keeping you stuck as described in the previous section. Emotion that is released in this way simply dissolves. You will completely liberate it from your energy field and from your inner self. As a result you will be amazed by how much energy you will have and how much better and lighter you will feel. Your health will begin to improve. You will have fewer colds and flu, less general illnesses, and you will have a lot more energy to do the things you want to do in your life. Energy multiplies energy. The more energy you have, the more energy you will produce. Then you will need to find an output for that energy - and this where you begin to raise your personal energy.

This is a building block of personal charisma. Charisma is when others find themselves compelled to listen to every word that you say. You stand out just because of the manner in which you express yourself. It's a very desirable quality to have. You acquire charisma because you have built and nurtured this energy in yourself. Drama is probably the most effective way of building this kind of expressive energy.

## R is for repetition

So we've come to the last and probably the most important element in the "from wallflower to sunflower journey": repetition. Almost everything you do - and everything you have ever done, that you now do naturally or automatically - is the result of repetition. If you only ever took one step, you would not learn to walk.

For a new behaviour pattern to become natural, it needs to be repeated over and over again. All the previous steps that we've talked about - the support; the understanding; the expression; the expansion; the energy; the freedom; the flow; being in touch with your intuition; transforming unconscious blocks - will become more effective when they are practiced regularly. This is why most of the courses I run take place over a period of time.

The Sunflower Effect works on all these levels, all at the same time, and this is what makes it so powerful. It's not a technique, not something you have to remember. Once it has become second nature, it's going to be there with you all the time. This is what is going to enable you to cross over the fast flowing river to where the sunflowers live. It will enable you, too, to meet and overcome the challenges that come to all of us from time to time - challenges that will deepen even further your self-confidence and self-esteem. Imagine if this could be fun, so it could be something that you look forward to. The more you look forward to it, the more effortless it will be and the faster progress you will make. Imagine coming back to be with a group of people, supporting each other and empowering each other to make the breakthroughs you each are wanting to make. As one person transitions into their sunflower, everyone else moves too.

The more you practice and experience the Sunflower Effect, the more your confidence will grow and the faster you will make progress. This is the making of your fully blossomed sunflower.

**Please note:** If you feel a bit overwhelmed by all you have read in this chapter, don't worry. As I've explained, all these things are happening at once and you probably won't be aware they are happening - as Owain discovered below. You don't need to understand how or why it's working. This is the beauty of the Sunflower Effect, and this is why the play and story aspects are so important - because they distract your mind so that, over time, deep change can take place.

## Owain

*Owain was a quiet, sensitive man who worked in I.T. with a capacity for deep thought and feeling. He described how he sat at his desk all day and often never moved from it. He felt he was living life in a straitjacket, compelled to follow certain routines and, over time, had found himself feeling afraid of moving out of these set routines, in case it was commented on or noticed by other people. This had made him feel increasingly remote from other people and increasingly unhappy.*

*Owain was amazed at the benefits he experienced as a result of participating in the Sunflower Effect, simply because he was getting more comfortable with expressive movement. He actually hadn't moved his body in a natural way for many years, except as part of one of his routines e.g. gym, exercise classes, travelling to work. His life just didn't require him to do this. As a sensitive man this, and the years of working in sterile office environments, had taken its toll on him and he had developed strategies for coping.*

Through the Sunflower Effect, he had reconnected with this instinctive part of himself and he found himself feeling freer to be himself at work. He started moving around his office and socialising with his colleagues. He hadn't learned a technique, he just naturally started doing these things. All his fears and limitations of behaving in this way had simply dissolved. He discovered that he was actually a natural communicator and had very good social skills. By the end of the course he had invited numerous work colleagues, including senior managers, to his birthday celebration - and they had responded very positively towards him. This was something he couldn't conceive of doing before the course. Thus he was effortlessly able to move from wallflower to sunflower in a relatively short space of time. The combination of his quiet personality and his alienating environment had created these issues, as are experienced by many people working in offices, particularly those working with computers.

In the next chapter I'll be explaining in more depth how the Sunflower Effect achieves these magical effects.

## Chapter 7

# The Fastest Way of Becoming a Sunflower

**Your magic power to break old habits and create new patterns of confident behaviour that's been with you from the beginning - but you didn't know it**

We have been working throughout this book with a metaphor of the sunflower growing. This is the same for you. You came into the world brimming with potential and destined to express this potential as a human being - even if you don't believe it because the experiences in your life that have caused you to doubt yourself.

In this chapter, I will be explaining the most important underlying principles that lie within the Sunflower Effect, which over time will enable you to unlock the hidden sunflower that lies dormant within you, and make this a reality. This will help you through the times when you doubt that the process is working for you, when your Resistor is coming up with clever ways to block you from making progress. Understanding these principles will enable your analytical mind to process your experience, and in some cases will actually make the Sunflower Effect work more effectively.

**Wired for story**

We are turning our attention to a different kind of metaphor - a story. A story is an extended metaphor that has two parallel levels.

The first level is the entertainment level. The second is at the unconscious level, which can bring about profound transformation, even to those deeply ingrained adaptive patterns and aspects of your personality that are keeping you locked away. Stories are powerful because they enable you to make sense of the overwhelming world around you.

According to Lisa's Cron's *Wired for Story* our brains think in story; we are hard-wired for story. This is why children love stories. From the moment their brains have matured enough they begin to create stories. It's actually how you developed as a human being and, if you know something about child psychology, you will be familiar with the different development stages that children go through. They play out and project their feelings onto their toys – and make stories using their toys as characters. This is the way they process their experiences and come to terms with feelings they don't understand. This is teaching them valuable lessons about life, which are going to enable them to endure hardships, overcome challenges, and motivate them to fulfil their potential.

It's the same for adults, but we may have lost touch with this ability, believing the brainwashing we have received that stories are pure entertainment, escapism, and not serious. However, our capacity to process our experiences and resolve our difficulties through story never leaves us. Sue Jennings' fascinating books describe this process in a lot more detail (see this book's website).

### Inbuilt into your psychology is the ability to transform through stories

It is inbuilt into your psychology to transform through stories. This is why the Sunflower Effect is so powerful, works so well and can effortlessly transform the deepest psychological blockages, even the ones you've struggled for years to make any progress on. This is because, unlike many talking approaches, the Sunflower Effect doesn't work through speaking about your formative experiences.

It works through stories: ancient stories that have fascinated us since time immemorial. Many of these stories have been retold and recreated by every generation. Many of them are the stories that you flock to cinemas to watch, or watch online, read in books, or read to your children at bedtime. The story-making business is not dying out; it's expanding. As humans we are inspired, entertained and delighted by stories. We become lost in a story. We escape from the difficult facts of our own lives into a story and immediately feel better. We are able to relax, let go of our stress, forget our latest upset and learn how other people cope with impossible situations. It's like reality and yet it's not reality. But our brains register it at the level of reality: as if it's really happening, as if it's really real. Have you come away from reading a powerful novel or from watching a film and felt full of your experiences, felt more alive, as if the events had actually happened to you? Your heart actually began to pump faster; you experienced a gamut of emotions, real emotions that you actually felt.

Humans have created stories from ancient times, simple ways of explaining their relationship to the world and the powerful things that have happened in history. All the old stories are stories of transformation; they take you on a journey into the character's deepest fears, and their capacity to meet and eventually to triumph over them (even the quiet, shy, reserved, oppressed or timid characters). Spiritual leaders, gurus and teachers communicate powerful messages through symbolic stories – as do politicians, speakers, authors, leaders and anyone else who has important information to communicate. They typically use stories that serve a double function: to entertain but also to inspire, enlighten and to bring about some kind of change in understanding.

These are the kind of stories that we use in the Sunflower Effect. These are stories that have a symbolic action; that bring into play unconscious learning; and break adaptive patterns. Such stories facilitate transformation and change. This is why working with these stories though the Sunflower Effect can really help to break those deep-rooted habitual patterns.

## Why ordinary stories on their own don't change you

Reading a book or watching a film rarely changes people's lives in a permanent way - although for a time, you may imagine that you are one of the actors or characters in the film or the book and aspire to be like them.

However, after a while, the effects of the film or book wear off and you return to normal life; and you're back to feeling those old familiar feelings again. But what if the film or book was even more like real life; as if you had really been the person in the film or the book and had achieved these things? Yes, the things that in your own life you have no hope of achieving because of your skill level, your personality or because you can't see yourself doing them. You'd be afraid of other people laughing at you, at seeing you as too big for your boots - if you suddenly started behaving like the actors in the film.

## Creating new patterns – forming new neuronal pathways

You make major change in your life when you start to behave in different ways and when you create **new neuronal pathways.** This is a neurological phenomenon that is built into your physiology that affects your psychology and the way you behave. We have been speaking in this book, about how difficult it is to break your adaptive patterns. If you keep on behaving in the same way you've always behaved, the same things keep happening; the same pattern keeps on being played out because you are following a neuronal pathway. This is what is keeping you stuck.

When a pattern is created and it has been repeated many times, it's very hard to stop repeating it. This can be seen in any kind of printing process. Wallpaper or textile manufacturers choose a pattern that they believe is going to delight their customers. Their machines print this pattern over and over again - the pattern will not change until it's replaced with a new pattern.

This is the same for you when you are seeking to behave in new way; you are seeking to create a new pattern. However this is not easy to do because, unlike the wallpaper manufacturers, it's often not easy to change the patterns that have been formed by your neuronal pathways.

This is why confidence-building techniques only work if you practice the technique over and over again, exactly as the technique was taught. This is what creates the new pattern and the new behaviour, which, by this time, has become second nature. The trouble is that most people don't practice the technique exactly as taught. They either forget important elements of the technique or they feel too embarrassed to deliver the technique as learned - because often it doesn't align with their personality or their normal behaviour.

You may have experienced this yourself. The technique felt so alien to you that you believed other people would see right through you – they'd instantly know you'd gone on a course and learned a new technique. Thus you fear that they might feel manipulated by you because you're practicing a technique on them. You want to avoid this and, since you feel so self-conscious, there's now more of a possibility that you'll fail to practice the technique as taught. Thus, in time, you'll return to your usual behaviour. However, learning a technique that improves existing behaviour may be very effective later on in your journey from wallflower to sunflower – because you will by then have the confidence to carry it off.

The Sunflower Effect rebuilds your new behaviour from the inside and doesn't require you to get it right. The Sunflower Effect offers a laboratory where you can experiment, where you can take risks and try out new behaviours in a safe environment. At first you will feel like a baby bird attempting to fly. Your "wings" will not be working very well but, through that activity, the baby bird is developing the muscles, the flexibility and strength that it needs to fly - just as you did when you were learning to walk. It doesn't matter that you're a novice at first, because you are developing the building blocks of what is going to become your new behaviour – and this is what helps to create new neuronal pathways.

## The most effective way of creating new patterns – and making long-lasting change

You may remember from my story that I was able to break my life-long pattern of being a wallflower through drama. In fact, I was not the drama type. I disliked the ego-driven culture of most amateur drama because I felt acutely self-conscious. I hated the competitive, superficial atmosphere that I perceived in most drama groups and, still to this day, I steer away from this. However, I was to discover a very different kind of drama that was collaborative and highly expressive, which enabled me to awaken hidden parts of myself that were keeping me on the sidelines. This was what, over time, enabled me to bring about major behavioural change. Since 1997, I've been teaching this to people with far less confidence than

I had and watched them make major shifts in their lives - shifts that they never believed were possible for them.

Drama enables you to play out the stories in films and novels **for real,** so you actually can become the hero. Actors who play out these characters have a gift of being able to convince the world that they are the character. It's about **being**. For me, what was so powerful in my early acting experiences was discovering that all I had to do was pretend - just as I had played "pretend games" when I was a child and it hadn't left me. It took me back to my bookworm days when, I was able to enter into the world of the main character of the novel I was reading through my imagination. I believed I *was* this character. I felt what they felt. In this way I was able to find that character in myself, however different they were from me. This is the building blocks of acting - imagining you are a character, feeling what they are feeling and doing what they're doing. It's as simple as that. This is the kind of drama that we explore in the Sunflower Effect.

### "I can't do drama!"

If you are thinking, "Drama! I can't do drama. I'll be the one person stuck on the sidelines, running for the door," I'll tell you the story of Linda, who declared at the beginning of one of my workshops that she was hopeless at drama.

### Linda

*"I felt so self-conscious, I couldn't get into character,"* Linda had explained. In fact, her experience had little to do with self-consciousness. Linda had felt totally overwhelmed by how very expressive the woman had been who had partnered her in the exercise. She was thus feeling disappointed with herself and believed she had failed.

*This is fairly typical. She had compared herself to her partner, judged herself and found herself wanting. Comparing yourself to other people is often the biggest block to your confidence and self-expression.*

At the next opportunity, I invited Linda to let go of her self-criticism and to free herself from any pressure to perform or "be good." I said, "Just imagine how that character is feeling and then let yourself be the character in your own way. It's not about acting, it's just about feeling."

Linda stopped trying to perform and started to really occupy the character and soon was showing a real aptitude for acting. This is all acting is - the capacity to step out of yourself and imagine yourself as another human being. Linda stopped feeling self-conscious and, through the day, she discovered more and more freedom to express herself. It was inspiring to see her letting herself go. Like her partner in the first exercise, she was having a ball and everyone else was enjoying the fact that she was having so much fun, particularly her first partner. She was receiving praise for playing these characters in her own way and this was bringing out hidden parts of self, parts of herself which had become locked away through recent experiences when she had lost confidence. She was freeing these shutdown parts of herself, the adaptive patterns, in which as humans we find a way of coping with a challenge. This adaptation is rarely ever healthy. It usually involves shutting down our vital energies. As a result of setting this part of herself free, Linda began to feel like a new person. She was being her "real self" and, at the same time, she was coming alive.

One of the things that I say to people, who are having difficulty with doing the drama, is, "Actors get paid to do this, and they sometimes get paid a lot of money for doing it." I invite them to imagine that they're being paid a very large sum of money for participating in the exercise. I suggest they choose a sum that would make a really big difference to their bank account. At the end of the exercise, I invite them to imagine they're receiving this money as payment for their services for the group. This is another way of rewarding themselves for their courage in taking a risk that was way out of their comfort zone.

Linda thought she wasn't good at drama. She was convinced that her performance had been bad and her partner's performance had been great. Therefore she was beating herself up, and in this resulted in self-criticism that led to her shutting down. In fact there was no "good" or "bad". "Good" and "bad" are terrible names for what had happened. They were both on different journeys - they were having different experiences and, as a result, learning different things.

If they had been going to different destinations. If one had been going to Timbuktu and the other to Transylvania, they wouldn't expect to have had the same experience, and yet most people think like this when it comes to any kind of performing situation. This is how you get hardwired into creating black and white distinctions between good and bad, right and wrong, success and failure. This can block you in your progress.

## Breaking the habit of self-consciousness

Once she stopped worrying about what other people were thinking about her, Linda could let herself go. She was able to open herself to the character's experience and she started really enjoying herself. The more she enjoyed herself, the easier it was for her to break her habitual pattern of self-consciousness. It happened naturally, without her thinking about. This is what enables new and more confident behaviour to emerge. Over time, as your new behaviour becomes your default mode, this will naturally be expressed in your outside life. Often it takes very little time for this to start taking effect. Many of my clients find the thought of the drama very difficult, particularly at the beginning. It's such an alien thing for them: to step out of themselves and to become someone else. They feel acutely self- conscious and are afraid that they'll freeze up and look foolish. Yet most did it with ease as children and this ability has not left them, just like riding a bike.

In a safe environment, where there is no shame for being frozen or paralysed, where other people are empathising with the experience of feeling frozen and might even be experiencing that themselves - it suddenly becomes OK to be frozen. It's just something that happened. Even though you may have felt acutely self-conscious and uncomfortable, it's very common that, the next time you tried it, you would be able to let go a little more, to participate a little more and to feel a little less self-conscious - a little less afraid of making a fool of yourself.

When this is repeated over and over again, your self-consciousness will finally fade away, and you may even find that you are enjoying yourself. There is just a little more space in you to relax and just give it a go and, as you do this, a lot of experiences in your outside life will become a lot easier.

## New behaviour

This is what in time leads to new behaviour: the confident behaviour of the sunflower. As a result of doing drama, I noticed I was no longer watching myself from the outside - one of the painful aspects of my wallflower experience which meant I was always standing guard outside myself, censoring everything I said and did. I hadn't been "at home" with myself: I had always been on the outskirts of myself, looking in.

Through drama, I was truly discovering how to be **inside myself**, and this was very different from my habitual mode. This is, paradoxically, what playing a character does. It had enabled me to access my authentic self, the natural confidence that lived in me even though I was a wallflower, see *The Self Confidence Myth* (Chapter 8). This had overridden my default mode of wallflower behaviour and created a new pattern - a new pattern that gradually had become my new default "sunflower" behaviour.

This enabled me to live much more in the present moment, less worried about repeating the mistakes of the past. I also found myself participating more, volunteering my opinion from time to time. I was amazed when others seemed to appreciate my viewpoint, and began to see me as one of the confident ones, the ones that spoke up and were thus remembered.

One of the most important watersheds in this change was the fact that, on stage, everyone was behaving in different ways towards me from how I experienced people behaving in my real life - when I was hanging around on the sidelines. They were doing this because the scenario required them to behave like this and this was setting up different social patterns in me. This was breaking my old pattern of being a wallflower in which people ignored me or behaved towards me in an undermining way.

What I didn't realise was that I had been **drawing this behaviour out of them** by behaving as a wallflower (with all the accompanying thought patterns and expectations of how other people **should** behave towards me). Whilst it appeared that they were excluding me or discounting me, actually **I was excluding and discounting myself** and they were picking up these unconscious messages, and **doing what I was unconsciously asking them to do.** When I stopped playing out this behaviour and putting out these unconscious messages, I started behaving more like the characters

I was playing in the dramatic situations, particularly the more empowered ones. I had, in effect, created a new neuronal pathway and broken an old behaviour pattern; as a result, I also started seeing significant changes in how other people were treating me.

When I experienced other people seeing me as powerful or dynamic or brave or inspiring in a dramatic situation, it was as if I was experiencing this in real life - and this enabled me to have very different experiences from my habitual ones. This was breaking old social roles and modes.

When other people start responding to you in different ways, you never forget it. You have broken the pattern that keeps you holding back, or keeps you afraid. In fact, your psychology (your unconscious) knows no difference between a real situation and a simulated situation, and the more emotionally involved you become in the situation the more real it feels.

I see this over and over again in my groups, with people whose life experience has caused them to believe that they are the quiet ones whom no one notices. Given the right setting and conditions, all kinds of gifts and qualities begin to emerge in them – qualities they didn't know they had. In fact these qualities were there all the time, but they were so deeply buried in the person, often because of depression, fear or anxiety, that it has been impossible to access them. All that is needed is the key to let them out. The most effective way of unlocking this key is through the magical power of drama.

## Vanitha

*Vanitha was a beautiful, young Indian girl with an affecting smile who was constantly seeking approval from other people. At work her colleagues were constantly taking advantage of her because she appeared sweet and timid. Inside, however, Vanitha was seething* and was fed up with her more dominant colleagues, who were abusing their position. Inside, she felt far from sweet and timid.

In an exercise, she found herself attracted to playing the vulnerable mother of the hero. Vanitha was surprised, as was everyone else, by the fervour with which she expressed the mother's emotions. She felt fantastic afterwards because she had been able to let out emotions that she was afraid of expressing in her everyday life - in case others rejected her. She discovered that she had a power within her that was an essential part of her personality. It was her drive to achieve things in her life.

Eventually she found a way of expressing this power, so that her work colleagues got to see this true part of herself, without needing to be aggressive or unpleasant. She just simply gave them a "look" the next time they tried to take advantage of her. It didn't lead to them rejecting her – in fact they liked and respected her more for it. And she never again had problems with her work colleagues.

This is like the sunflower that is shaded from the sun and is not able to thrive. Yet given a little bit of sunlight this sunflower will soon begin to grow and blossom. Thus, coming away from the sidelines and allowing yourself to be seen, will, instead of being intensely exposing, bring you alive and enable you to flourish, as Vanitha had done.

## Why you don't change when you really want to

It takes courage to change, and you are on a path of change because you are reading this book. You are changing as you are reading and you have now reached Chapter 7.

But has this ever happened to you? You've made a dramatic breakthrough in an area of your life and for a while that breakthrough really feels significant. You begin to get excited about how different your life is going to be from now on. Then slowly you find yourself slipping back into that old pattern or behaviour - and it's as if the breakthrough never happened. You are back a year later exactly where you started. It's quite common that people who win the lottery or acquire a large sum of money and believe it will change their lives, end up a few years later in exactly the same situation as before they received their windfall - living hand to mouth.

There are several very good reasons for this and understanding this, will save you any amount of heartache. It will stop you from beating yourself up or believing that what you've been doing to bring about change hasn't worked for you. The reason that you don't change often, is because you're not aware of **the powerful part of you that doesn't want to change**, that is resistant to change and will dig its heels in at the prospect of any real change happening in your life. This part lives in everyone.

The Resistor is the primitive part of you, your inbuilt defense system, which I have been speaking about in this book. It is responsible for a lot of your behaviours that make no sense; it resists change and is trying to protect you from change because it wants to keep you safe (or so it believes). The Resistor loves familiar things and distrusts new experiences. So, even if the familiar thing is very uncomfortable and the new thing very positive, it will still gravitate to the familiar thing. This is expressed very powerfully in the image of a baby being held by a warm-hearted nurse who's still crying out to be with the mother who had abused him, rather than the nurse who's given him love and care. At some level this is happening in everyone at the prospect of significant change.

This part of you is permanently on guard against change. **It's like the soldier who is still fighting a war that ended years ago.** There is nothing more potentially disruptive in the Resistor's mind than change. The bigger the change, the harder the Resistor will defend its territory.

## Payoffs: the Resistor's seduction game

The Resistor is crafty. It will give the illusion that it has accepted change, because it knows how to play the system but it's "acting on orders" to resist. Nothing is going to stop the Resistor from carrying out those orders.

One of the Resistor's strategies is to create powerful pay-offs. These are the false "perks" of being a wallflower – all the thing you get out of being a wallflower that you've become very attached to. The Resistor warns you that change involves letting go of those pay-offs and so it's much better to stay the way you are. Here are some of mine. The more I stepped into my power and became more of my true self, my Resistor believed:

- The more people would dislike me
- The more people would misunderstand me
- I'd have to let go of my "nice girl" image
- My failures would become more public
- There's lots of things I wouldn't get away with anymore
- Others would expect more of me and judge me more
- Others would look at me and expect me to set an example
- I would feel more exposed in lots of situations
- Members of my family wouldn't recognise me any more and would try to get the old Claire back
- I would lose good friends.

All these erroneous beliefs were keeping me unconsciously locked into my wallflower identity. Most of the things that I feared would happen either didn't happen or posed little threat to me when they did and, at times, were positive steps in my transformation. I did lose friends but I rapidly acquired a whole host of new friends who were more on my wavelength and far more supportive. As I became more confident and therefore more visible to others, when someone appeared to dislike me, I saw it as a sign of progress and even rather revelled in the fact. I no longer needed to be liked by everyone and the people I respected liked me more - because I was being authentic.

They even liked what I had previously considered my "bad bits."

**Exercise: your payoffs**

What are yours? Jot them down in your notebook. It's very powerful to name these pay-offs. You will probably find there are one or two that really get you; and where losing approval in those areas is going to be really tough.

The Resistor is devious and will cloak resistance in the most subtle of ways. Often it's just a feeling of dread or numbness that persists whenever you think about the change, which goes away as soon as you decide to delay or postpone the proposed change. Notice when an opportunity for change shows up but all kinds of "reasons" then surface as to why you can't move forward on this trajectory. These are some of the typical ones:

- It's not convenient i.e. timing or geography.
- Changes or potential changes to your finances, job, availability etc.
- Other people's disapproval or situations i.e. family, friends
- Belief you can do it on your own.
- You won't have the energy

You now have a choice point: whether to give into your Resistor and its tempting payoffs or to move forward on your journey from wallflower to sunflower.

## The courage to change when you don't really want to change

Thus one of the most important stages in the process of change is **recognising that at a deep level you don't want to change.** When you take responsibility for your Resistor in this way, that's the moment when you are truly opening up a pathway for **real change.**

There's an exercise in one of my courses where you have the opportunity play out your Resistor, as if it was a real person. In actual fact, it's a very plausible and human-like part of your psychology, framed as the "Chimp" by Prof Steve Peters in his book *The Chimp Paradox*. You will discover what makes your Resistor tick, what motivates your Resistor, and what will disarm it. You get to play out your internal interactions with your Resistor, so you can see what tactics influence the Resistor. You will also know when your Resistor is running you, so you can be alert to its manipulations and strategies. If you're going to outwit your Resistor, you've got to be just as crafty. You will need to use subterfuge and stealth to bring about a shift in your inbuilt defence system that resists transformation. The Resistor will relax when there doesn't seem to be any threat to the system. This is one of the reasons I believe, many head-based and verbal solutions to confidence building don't work long-term - because they are relying on conscious, logical methods. Immediately the Resistor hears that change is in the offing, it's on the alert to protect the system from attack. And although it may let some small change get through, it's going to be working out a strategy to banish those disruptive and unwanted elements.

When the Resistor believes there is nothing serious going on, it relaxes. This is one of the reasons why the Sunflower Effect is so effective at bringing about radical change: see Letting Go in the previous chapter. Because the Sunflower Effect works through story and play, as described in this chapter and the next two chapters, this distracts the conscious and unconscious mind. This will allow the deeper work to go on without any interference, enabling you to free the emotions and blockages that have been buried at an unconscious level.

## The Resistor as your ally

In truth, your Resistor is your ally. It's your pathway to awakening the hidden sunflower that lies dormant within you, if you know how to shift its negative action into positive support.

In the next two chapters, you will be seeing how the Sunflower Effect works in practice. You, too, will have the opportunity to experience this for yourself in the fourth bonus of this book. This will take you on a profound journey into your inner self in which you will be discovering your Secret Weapon, a powerful transformational tool to outwit your Resistor; though which you will be able to effect your transition from wallflower to sunflower.

## Chapter 8
# Your Secret Weapon to Building Lasting Confidence

**Why it can be so hard to build lasting self-confidence - and how to overcome your toughest obstacles**

It's not easy to move from wallflower to sunflower, for all the reasons explained so far in this book. In this chapter, we will be working with the story of the Japanese sun goddess, Amaterasu (the phonetic pronunciation, Amat-er-a-su) so you can get a sense of how working with a story through the Sunflower Effect, as described so far, can indeed, facilitate the transition from wallflower to sunflower in a relatively short time. More importantly, you will also be discovering how to unlock the Secret Weapon, which will, in time, enable you to disarm your Resistor and thus overcome the internal blockages to building the lasting confidence that so far has eluded you.

**Your potential to become a fully blossomed sunflower**

I have chosen to work with the story of Amaterasu, since it mirrors the journey of transformation from wallflower to sunflower and brings you to the point of revelation, as Amaterasu emerges back into the world and shines her light on everyone. At this point she becomes a fully blossomed sunflower, because that's what she is and always was. This is the same for you.

Each and every one of us is born an Amaterasu. You were born brimming with that potential to become a fully blossomed sunflower - you had that potential sunflower in you long before you even came into the world. The journey of Amaterasu is principally a way of connecting with the part of you that is willing to shine or is, right now, ready to step out of the shadows and into the sunlight. This is your true Amaterasu and is the means by which you will be able to counteract the part of you that is programmed to contract: so you can create a new programme and thus a new way of being in the world. In time, you will be able to step into your potential and become the person you've always wanted to be - the sunflower who is confident and happy, just the way you are.

Indeed, Amaterasu shines her light because if she didn't do this, there would be no light. She would be depriving the world of something that is vitally important. The sun is the source of all, the source of nature, constantly replenishing itself - it sustains the light and everything that lives and breathes. Amaterasu is the fullest expression of the sunflower that lives in you. She shines her light because that's what she does. It's what she is. She has never been anything else. It's quite simply her job, just as it's your birthright to shine your light and fulfil your potential.

### Exercise: accessing your sunflower

You will now have an opportunity to explore Amaterasu in further depth and to connect with your potential to become a fully blossomed sunflower. Listen to Audio 1 of Bonus 4 to participate in this exercise. The Bonus 4 exercises will take you on a profound journey into your inner self exploring the cast of characters that live within you: through exploring the characters in this story. In so doing, you will be working with your **internal theatre** and the deeper causes that have been keeping you stuck, which have been causing you so much unnecessary stress and suffering. In this process, you will be discovering your Secret Weapon by which you can distract your internal defence system and outwit your Resistor.

Listening to the audios will take you out of your analytic mind and into the deeper wisdom of your unconscious awareness. It will allow you to experience the characters' story as if it was really happening to you, with the help of your imagination (even if you don't think you've got one).

## The too perfect sibling

All would be perfect for Amaterasu; however, as for most of us, life is not perfect for Amaterasu. She has a brother, Susanno, the storm god and all Susanno wants to do is to destroy her. Susanno loves chaos and creating havoc; this is his function as a storm god. He derives pleasure out of sending rain, thunder and lightning, destroying anything that comes close to him. When he sees Amaterasu, something inside him just flicks a switch. He can't bear the way she's always so loving - she's always smiling and she's always so happy shining her light on everyone. And he can't stand the fact that everybody loves her - nobody seems to appreciate him so he starts getting resentful.

He starts to look for ways to upset her. First, he does one thing, then he tries another, then he does another thing, and when she doesn't react again - he comes up with the one thing that is **really, really going to upset her.**

In this story, Amaterasu is playing out the too-perfect sibling pattern in which one brother or sister is "really lovely," and everyone loves such a child because they are so loving, so good, so perfect in every way. But then the other sibling feels jealous and wants to destroy the good one. Certain families play out this pattern in which one sibling wages war on the other, and, instead of this bringing out the true self in the lovely sibling, they become even more perfect. Perhaps you've had a brother or sister who's like Susanno, or maybe it shows up in other relationships: a partner, people at work; other family members; even friends who play out this pattern in some way and seem out to get you, for no apparent reason.

The Amaterasu in the family is so alienated by the destructive behaviour of their sibling that they swear that they are never going to behave in this way, and so they bury these parts of themselves and deny they feel like this. However, at the same time, they so fully absorb the destructive force of their Susanno sibling that they become deeply traumatised. But they are good at hiding that too.

This is one of the many causes of the "too good child" pattern, who then becomes frozen in their goodness and terrified of letting their true self out in case they lose the love they have. They don't know what unconditional love is, even if it was available to them, because they have built their own conditions and now their hands are tied. I was one of those too good children.

## Why it can be so hard to move from wallflower to sunflower

In truth we all have a Susanno within us that wants to destroy us. This may seem unbelievable to you. It's not logical. It's what is called in psychology the Shadow, the parts of you that are hidden away, unseen and unknown. This is another reason why it can be very hard to move from wallflower to sunflower by traditional confidence- building methods.

Susanno/the Shadow is also the nasty children at school who behaved in a destructive way towards you; or the challenging people at work who seem out to get you, as in the case of

Vanitha in the previous chapter. The Shadow may turn up in certain relationships (partners, friends, family etc), and it may even be a recurring theme in your life. It's also the negative voice inside your head that won't shut up: the voice that keeps repeating all the negative things you've heard from other people, along with the things that other people wouldn't dream of **ever** saying to you. The Resistor, as explained in the previous chapter, is also an aspect of the Shadow: your defence system that stops you from making positive changes in your life.

Susanno is a storm god. Storms create terrible damage to the earth, yet storms are also nature's way of reducing pressure build-up, just as expressing angry feelings releases psychological pressure. If too much pressure builds up, then there is an explosion: an earthquake, a volcano, a tidal wave, an avalanche etc. Storms are necessary. They maintain the balance of life just as the sun does. This is why you need to express Susanno/the Shadow in your life as much as you need to express Amaterasu - but in a **healthy** way.

Susanno wants to destroy Amaterasu. He can't help himself. He is the full expression of the opposing energies in nature that maintain balance. The storm god occludes the sun goddess in the same way as storm clouds occlude the sun. The storm god is dancing. As thunder threatens, rain falls and lightning strikes, he is enjoying himself, playing his game, doing what he does best – storm and rage. This is why it's so positive to express Susanno's energy through the adapted form of drama used in the Sunflower Effect, in which it's safe and acceptable to express anger, rage and destructiveness, without causing pain or distress to others. You will even be rewarded for it – since actors are applauded for expressing these emotions. As we have seen, these emotions are the ones that most wallflowers have learned to suppress. This is why the Sunflower Effect is so effective at shifting the patterns that are keeping you locked in disempowering behaviours, which are a direct result of emotional suppression.

## The fastest way of becoming a sunflower

Paradoxically, it's the mechanism of the Shadow that is going to enable you to build the lasting confidence you are seeking, so you can easily transition from wallflower to sunflower. In fact it's going to greatly speed up your progress. As horrible and horrific you may feel your Shadow is, or the Susanno-type people who keep on showing up in your life, when you get to the bottom of what makes your Shadow tick, you will find a very powerful part of you. This is the part that's lain hidden and buried in you - maybe for the whole of your life. Thus the fastest way of becoming a sunflower is by accessing the **power of your Shadow.**

In this chapter you will be discovering how to harness this power, and unlock your Secret Weapon for creating radical shifts in your confidence levels, which will enable you to step into your fully blossomed sunflower. One of the strengths of the Sunflower Effect is that it will enable you to marshal the resources of your Shadow, and for most people this is also enormous fun.

Like your Resistor, your Shadow is your greatest ally. It can work **for** you as well as against you. It holds your power and your potential. It is pure gold. It's as powerful as the energy of Amaterasu, and in some ways more powerful, because it's a negative power. When you play out your Shadow consciously for the purpose of transformation, this energy begins to turn in the other direction. It's like a massive warship turning around; it may take a huge amount of effort to turn that warship around, but when it does, instead of fighting against you, **it's fighting for you.**

## The secret power of villains

Paradoxically you love your Shadow, even when it's doing terrible things to you. You can't help yourself. It's the same force in you, just like when you love to hate a villain. Villains in a heist film are so clever in their villainy that even their opponents admire the brilliance of their game. Blockbuster films that attract large audiences owe their success to the presence of a formidable villain, monster or destructive force that is deeply feared and creates dramatic tension. As viewers, you may find yourself both hating and loving this kind of villain, just as you love and hate your own Shadow - at one moment on their side and the next gunning for their downfall. This is the same admiration you have for an opponent you loathe but who brings out your fighting spirit and ultimately the best in you. There is often a very thin line between hate and love. It's another one of those paradoxes.

Young children both love and hate monsters for this same reason. If you ask them about monsters, they will either light up and are excited by all that is horrible about the monster or they will have a strong reaction: terror, disgust, hatred, wanting to fight the monster etc. But if a child is scared by a monster, their response is very different from an adult's. Children do not try to hide the fact they are scared. They are open about it and so there is also enjoyment of the fear. It becomes a game and an opportunity for play.

Perhaps you remember a game when you were a child, when someone played a monster and you ran away screaming. Part of the pleasure is being absolutely terrified that the monster is going to get you, but absolutely loving it when the monster finds you and eats you up. This is a way in which children come to terms with their negative power, an expression of their own Shadow that they do not yet understand; however, at some level they know how important it is.

The villain, monsters and the challenging people in your life are Shadow Projections. They are expressions of the negative power within you that you can't come to terms with, so you project it into the outside world and onto the villains that you really hate; the villains that you love to hate; and the people in your life who you battle with and who you dislike or loathe. You believe they are the complete antithesis of who you are and yet psychology says that's not entirely true. In fact they are a deeply buried part of you that you deny.

It's the negative force within you that's blocking you from making the progress you desire, however hard you work at it. This is the key to unlocking this part of you and eventually freeing yourself. You may already be familiar with the concept of the Shadow but this still is not enabling you to make the shift. This is probably because you are only relating to your Shadow at a head level (by talking about it) or you are only seeing it as purely negative. This is what is keeping you stuck. You don't yet know it deeply, as a potent and transformational aspect of your psychological make-up. This is what you are about to discover.

### Playing nasty characters – your secret weapon for building lasting confidence

When I started playing nasty, bad or immoral characters in drama I was able to work with this part of myself at a deep level - without realising this is what was happening. I was able to reclaim parts of myself that I had suppressed or disowned and so begin to reverse the effects of the too-good child who had become a too-nice adult.

I actually found playing villains and powerful characters hugely enjoyable. It gave me permission for being bad whilst being rewarded for playing the villain. As we have seen, the villain gets just as much applause as the hero, and indeed sometimes more – since playing the villain can be more stretching for an actor, and can require a deeper level of skill. In playing the villain you can access more of these parts of yourself, and draw on more of your untapped resources. This is what makes the difference and enables these characters to become a powerful, transformational tool: see Stefan's account of playing the evil king at the end of the next chapter. Playing villains are, in fact, your Secret Weapon for building lasting confidence. It's "secret" because the powerful psychological effects are hidden from view and you are unaware of what's happening at an unconscious level.

Playing nasty characters can also be enormous fun, though maybe not at first, because drama and acting are alien activities for most wallflowers. But as you begin to learn the language of drama, it gradually becomes more and more fun until finally, it becomes a tool to liberate yourself from everything that's been holding you back. An accountant by profession, who had been searching for many years for a solution to the unhappiness that had always been with him, made this observation:

*I felt like I was simply engaging in innocent play with the other participants, laughing and having fun, while not realising that the process was stirring up the patterns in my subconscious that were keeping me stuck and unhappy. It wasn't until the end that I suddenly realised a deep change had occurred and experienced feelings of freedom, inner peace, and wholeness that had eluded me for many years.*

## Enactment of Amaterasu and Susanno

Susanno is as much a pathway to becoming a sunflower, as is Amaterasu. He is the other side of the coin – the dark side. Many sunflowers have dark centres, since the tiny florets that produce their sunflower seeds are dark. The Chinese yin-yang symbol recognises the necessary opposition and harmony of dark and light, negative and positive. As with the principles of electricity, the opposition of a positive and negative charge produces energy.

Playing out Susanno (or any other villain) is one of the most powerful expressions of the Sunflower Effect. It works through embodiment and allows **expression of energy.** It creates **opening**, stretches you out of your comfort zone and gives you permission to let your **outrageous** side out, opening up the pathway for **expansion** and freedom. It reverses programming in which you believed it was **wrong** to express negative emotion and, in the process, you'll be able to let go of suppressed and buried emotion that is keeping you depressed, constricted and inhibited. At the same time, this is moving unconscious blocks so you can start to dissolve the adaptive patterns that have been keeping you a wallflower. This is where the Sunflower Effect takes psychological theory out of the head into a potent, active transformation system.

When participants play out Amaterasu and Susanno, they have an opportunity to notice how they feel as each character. They may find one character particularly difficult or particularly enjoyable. This is an internal exercise, not a performance; an opportunity to discover aspects of themselves that they are not aware of in their everyday life. Playing out both characters in relationship to each other is often very telling. Many are surprised at how they felt as Amaterasu in relationship with Susanno, or vice versa. Here are some typical reactions:

*I couldn't stand the way Amaterasu kept shining and smiling. I wanted to wage war against her and it felt really good.*

*I felt completely helpless as Susanno. Whatever I did Amaterasu kept on shining. She was the more powerful one.*

*Susanno reminded me of my parent/sibling/teacher/boss. It was great to stand up to him for once and feel I wasn't afraid of him/her.*

*I felt so good and so powerful as Amaterasu. I felt as if I could do anything. I wasn't frightened of Susanno. I was enjoying playing with him.*

For some, the relationship between Amaterasu and Susanno feels very familiar and you may recognise experiences from past relationships. Emotions and memories may be triggered but, this time, you're not in the situation - so you'll find yourself expressing emotions in the dramatic situation that you're not able to express in your everyday life. People who normally avoid conflict often relish the opportunity to be confrontational in this exercise: this is a sign that a dormant aspect of their expression is wanting to be expressed. It can be very powerful for someone who has played the role of Amaterasu predominantly in their lives, to take on the role of Susanno.

## Ben

*Ben was a very quiet, sensitive man who suffered from anxiety. He was finding it hard to assert himself at work and, although he knew he was good at his job, more dominant but less talented people were getting promotion. He had been bullied at school and he had never really got over this.*

*He had great fun costuming himself as Susanno and sending thunder bolts with the drum down onto the earth. Having permission to really let himself go, he was surprised how much he* enjoyed this exercise and how good he felt. He made as much noise as he possibly could and he had enormous fun. He was never allowed to make noise as a child. He had always been afraid of his masculine energy and felt it was not OK for him to express himself, particularly as he had a very dominant, aggressive father.

Ben found he really loved playing these characters. He found he could express emotions very easily through this and he surprised himself at how well he was able to play such characters. This, of course, was highly significant.

He went on to join several other of my courses, where he got a real opportunity to express many different characters. As a result he started to find appropriate ways of expressing his stronger feelings in a way that was acceptable for others. Though still a sensitive man, he began to earn respect and recognition at work.

## Susanno's trump card

In the myth, Susanno begins to slip into deviant expression – and he goes too far. He is angry with Amaterasu: he is resentful and jealous. But he also feels full of self-hatred, guilt, rage and shame for feeling like this: just like most people do. Naturally he wants to hide those parts of himself, but the more he tries to hide them, the stronger they become. Anything that's suppressed becomes more powerful; and the longer it stays below ground the more pressure builds up. Over time, it will take on the proportions of a volcano. When volcanic matter is exposed to enormous pressure created by all this suppression, there comes a point when suddenly there is an eruption. This is what happens within Susanno. He erupts and he finds the thing that he knows is really going to upset Amaterasu. It cannot fail.

He throws a skinned horse into her sacred abode, her Weaving Hall where she is weaving the Fabric of the Universe with her women. This scene is a key scene in the myth. It's a sensitive moment for both characters but particularly for Amaterasu. This is an enormous shock to her, as Susanno finally finds a way of breaking through and utterly devastating her. This scene mirrors the traumatic experience that drove the wallflower onto the sidelines. This is why working with this story is so effective at bringing about major transformation to the blocks that are keeping you stuck as a wallflower.

### Exercise: Your Secret Weapon to lasting confidence

You will now have an opportunity to explore Susanno and the aspect of your Shadow that is most prominent in your life right now (and your Secret Weapon to lasting confidence), by listening to Audio 2 of Bonus 4. When you own the parts of you that feel like Susanno, this will enable you to access the power, magnificence and freedom that lies within this vital aspect of your psychology.

When you find your Susanno, you own your Shadow projections and you empower yourself. Susanno is the pure gold in you – not just your darkness but also your light. It is both the light and the dark of the sunflower that will enable you, in time, to give full expression to your deepest potential as a human being. Do this exercise when other people are behaving in a negative way towards you; or when you feel blocked; or are encountering obstacles. When you recognise that people or anything in the outside world, that appears to be destructive towards you, are all part of that same internal battle - you own your Shadow at a whole new level.

If you stay in your Amaterasu too long, all the intensity that goes into shining and doing good in the world will begin to have a de- energising and disempowering effect. You need some balance. You need a bit of the dark. Everyone needs this, and if you don't express this part of yourself you will become leaden, deadened and stuck in being too good/too perfect. Playing this energy out in a safe way is liberating and will enable you to reclaim your lost power.

The Shadow is, of course, to be found in the many thousands of villains in films, literature, plays, myths and fairy stories as described in this book. Playing out these characters through the Sunflower Effect, or other similar methods, is your Secret Weapon to creating long- lasting confidence and choosing another way of being in relationship with this part of yourself. Enjoy the exercise.

In the next few sections you will be discovering how working with Amaterasu and Susanno plays out for real.

## Amaterasu - the key to releasing family trauma

### Karen

*Karen had suffered enormous family trauma, which she had mainly put behind her - but she was struggling in her career and she was having some vocal problems, which she hadn't been able to resolve.*

*Karen found herself strongly drawn to play Amaterasu in the scene where Sussanno throws the skinned horse into Amaterasu's sacred weaving hall. However, instead of being shocked and running away as Amaterasu does, Karen felt a strong impulse to push Susanno away. This had been agreed between her and the other members of her group, as she had always been passive in her family. She strongly felt she needed to take a more active role. However, when the man who was playing Susanno threw the piece* of fabric that had been chosen to represent the skinned horse, a very remarkable thing happened.

It wasn't as if Karen pushed him very hard, but the man found himself staggering back until he finally fell against a Victorian French window. In normal circumstances this extremely thick, plate-glass window would have withstood the impact but, in this case, it shattered into pieces. The man, however, had not been hurt and had not felt that he had been pushed particularly violently. He just felt very surprised, as Karen did.

Karen knew exactly what this was. It was the force of stored anger that had been covertly expressed during this symbolic enactment. It was all the anger that she had buried and kept very tight within her and held in her vocal chords, making it hard for her to express herself.

I can vividly remember the expression on her face. It was stormy but completely self-contained. This was not the freely expressed rage of a character from Greek drama. This was anger that had had to be constrained and held in check. The shattered window was visual evidence to her of just how deep her anger was.

After the course Karen reported significant positive effects. But the next time I saw her, I was amazed at the change in her. This quiet, reserved woman, who was often overlooked, had become vibrant and alive. When she walked into a room, people noticed her and instantly warmed to her. She had become a fully blossomed sunflower. She attributed this dramatic change to the time when she had played Amaterasu and broken the window, when she was able to release the longstanding, unconscious rage that she had held-in for so long. It had happened in only a few seconds.

Karen had expressed both Amaterasu and Susanno together. No longer the too-perfect Sun Goddess, Karen as Amaterasu had expressed her stormy side.

## Susanno: the key to unlocking disempowering behaviour

For some people, the internal Susanno/Amaterasu dynamic can be extremely subtle. Exploring this dynamic can reveal keys to what is keeping you locked in disempowering behaviours and situations.

## Eugenia

*Eugenia knew she was very angry but she couldn't feel it. Her boss had told her that her anger was a problem and she had to do something about it. She was very reluctant to join the course because she had a highly analytical mind and she wasn't convinced it would solve her problems.*

*Eugenia found herself enjoying playing both Susanno and Amaterasu. Playing Amaterasu enabled her to find her soft, feminine side but she relished being more spiky as Susanno. She felt a release from expressing Susanno, sending storms onto the earth: but she could also feel herself holding back. The rigidity in her was very strong.*

*This, she later recognised, was her critical mother who was always finding fault and insisted on perfection. Nothing was ever good enough for her mother and Eugenia had repressed her rage and frustration, which had become so deeply buried in her she didn't know it was there. It was the only power she had had as a child, and had resulted in passive aggression that her mother was impervious to.*

*At the time, we were exploring some of the situations at work where she was coming into conflict with her boss, and it became apparent that her boss was mirroring her mother's behaviour and triggering a reactive response in her. She was responding to his critical style of communication, in the same way as she had learned to respond to her mother, and it was coming out through*

**passive anger.** Eugenia was totally unaware of this anger, because like Karen, it was held tightly in check.

Playing Susanno had enabled her to let go of some of this repressed energy. It had been enjoyable and had enabled her to free herself from the destructive effects of her own internal rage. She couldn't do anything about her boss's critical mode of communication, but she could do something about her own – given that she needed to do something about this fast so it was no longer sabotaging her relationship with her boss.

Because her rage was so deep, I realised it was going to take her a while to release its destructive power. She needed to do far more work with her Susanno before she could fully release the rage that was buried deep within her. So I suggested that she connect with the energy she had found in Amaterasu. The transformation in her communication was quite remarkable. She stopped being defensive and reactive, and started communicating her point from an empowered position. This made a radical difference to how her communication was received by others, and gave her the means to start building new communication bridges with her boss.

Many wallflowers experience **passive anger.** They are perceived as nice, kind, quiet, passive, easy, unthreatening, a walkover, a doormat and non-confrontational: but this is far from the whole truth. They have suppressed their anger, along with many other negative feelings. This anger becomes so deeply buried that they are often unaware that they are even feeling angry.

Other people are often aware of passive anger as Eugenia's boss was. However this kind of anger is commonly so deeply buried that other people will start feeling or expressing anger - without realising it doesn't belong to them. Many wallflowers are shocked by the negative behaviour of others towards them, not realising it's their own unexpressed anger being projected back to them. When I started releasing my unexpressed anger through drama, I noticed that other people started treating me in a more respectful way. I was no longer attracting negative people and disempowering behaviour that had previously been such an unpleasant feature of my life.

The truth is that when you blame somebody else or perceive them as the "enemy", the "bad one", the "problem", the "Susanno" - you put yourself in the place of the victim. This can be difficult to spot since most people feel more powerful when they are blaming or judging others. However this is a trap that will keep you stuck in perpetuating these disempowering situations.

Do you want to be a victim, or do you want to be a hero? A hero does not blame others; a hero just recognises there is a challenge so that he/she can take appropriate action. When you recognise that Susanno, and the people in the outside world that appear to be destructive towards you, are all part of the internal battle that we have been exploring in this chapter, then you move into the Hero. When you do this, you access your natural power and ability to transform many of the disempowering situations that have previously eluded you.

## Overcoming resistance

Playing out the Shadow calls into play aspects of your Resistor, your defence system, which is blocking you from making the changes you want to in your life. These in turn are blocking your confidence levels and also sabotaging any change that you are so close to achieving.

The Shadow does this by triggering your adaptive patterns (your habitual behaviours) deeply buried in the unconscious, which have built powerful psychological walls within you. These are the walls that you feel when you try to break away from the sidelines. Your Shadow can keep you stuck for years. You may have experienced this, and the frustration that can ensue when you can't make progress, or when you make little bits of progress and then get stuck.

I've seen this played out many times in my groups, with people who are highly motivated to bring about change but find themselves coming up against a brick wall – which they feel powerless to do anything about.

**Tracy**

*Tracy was really struggling in one of my courses. As much as she wanted to free herself of self-consciousness, as the course went on, she started to slip back. She saw other people making progress, and instead of building on the progress that she had made, she believed that everyone else was doing better than her and that she was the one person that the course wasn't going to work for. As a result she began to despair, and this further sabotaged her growing confidence.*

*Her "Susanno" had her in a vicious hold of critical thoughts and she was stuck in this vicious circle. Her Susanno was winning the battle and he didn't have to do much to send her hurtling back to square one. Critical patterns of thinking were so deeply ingrained in her that she was unaware of how she was disempowering herself. She was expending a huge amount of energy in "trying to change" and she was getting nowhere fast. Her impasse lay in one simple word: "trying" (and other words like it) that was keeping her in the struggle of fighting a losing battle.*

*It was within her power to transform how she described her experience, and instead to start using empowering language.*

*This was not easy as it was an ingrained habit to use such words, but when she did this she noticed that she stopped doubting herself and was able to follow through and access more confident aspects of herself.*

When you find your Susanno, you find that bit in you that is destructive towards yourself: you begin to find freedom.

In the next chapter, the most important chapter in this book, we will be turning our attention back to Amaterasu and the climatic moment of her story. This is too the **breakthrough point** in your own journey from wallflower to sunflower, when you will have the opportunity, through the remaining audios, to play out the final part of Amaterasu's story and, in so doing, step away from the shadows and move to where the sunflowers live.

## Chapter 9

# It's Your Turn to Shine

**Moving out of the shadows to the place where the sunflowers (the confident people) live**

The journey from wallflower to sunflower is a journey through the darkness into the light. However, this is a different darkness from the Shadow that Susanno represents. This is the darkness that lies within - the darkness that is almost unfathomable. It goes very deep, into the very core of us. It's the darkness that even the goddess of Ultimate Light retreats to when she is in darkness herself.

### Amaterasu's retreat

**Amaterasu is so shocked by Susanno's action when he throws a skinned horse into her Sacred Weaving Hall, that all she can do is to run.**

This is a natural psychological response to a traumatic experience. This is also what drives the wallflower into hiding. In a state of grief, in crisis, when the fear gets too much or when the world falls apart - **Amaterasu and the wallflower retreat.** All humans do. In the private, silent place of the Heavenly Rock Cave, there is the possibility of restitution. There, Amaterasu can come to terms with her experience so that, in time, she can find herself again.

The truth is that, even though Amaterasu withdraws into the cave, she doesn't stop being all the things we described in the previous chapter. She still has all that potential in her. However, there's a big price on Amaterasu's withdrawal - without the sun goddess the world begins to die. This is a story, that's told in many different ways in cultures all over the world, to explain natural phenomena. Imagine the fear that ancient people experienced when the sun first disappeared when it should have been shining; they must have truly feared that the light had gone forever.

This is also how you feel when you withdraw into the shadows.

You may have said to yourself at some time:

*"Am I ever going to come out of here? Am I ever going to cross the divide between me and other people? I know I brought myself to this place, but now I can't escape from it."*

You've retreated to your place of safety, to your Heavenly Rock Cave, and you're reluctant to come out of it. Amaterasu is afraid to leave the cave and of history repeating itself, she's maybe afraid of Susanno hanging around the mouth of the cave with another skinned horse (or someone like him exhibiting similar destructive behaviour). However, the fear of what is out there is often greater than the reality. In doing this, you and Amaterasu deprive the world of what you have to give. Amaterasu is depriving the world, and herself, of her own light: because now the Sun Goddess herself is in darkness. This is not natural to her. It's totally alien territory, **but she is safe.**

## Lessons from the cave

Now imagine being one of the people on earth who was used to seeing the sunrise on the horizon and its ascension up to the heavens. But now there is no light; there is no sunshine, only darkness. They sit in the darkness, waiting for the light. They wait and they wait, huddling together for warmth – because, without the sun warming the earth, it's terribly cold. They long for the light to come, for the day to come, and this interminable night, this interminable waiting, to stop. There's not much they can do in the inky blackness, waiting and hoping that the light will come back. They have to face this darkness and being in perpetual night. This is how it feels when you've locked yourself away in the cave; you cannot do many of the things you want to do.

If you could imagine being Amaterasu, you would probably enjoy being in the darkness for a while. You may find yourself enjoying living without Susanno. At this moment he can no longer annoy you, he's no longer trying to upset you - and maybe you begin to enjoy wondering what he might be doing without you: *"Is he missing me? How is the world is getting on whilst I'm in here, out of it all – no longer needing to shine my light on the world?"*

It's getting boring, but this is not the kind of boredom that enables Amaterasu to do something about it. This is a deathly boredom. In fact, Amaterasu gets so bored that she begins to lose interest in being out there, in rejoining the world and shining her light. She begins to believe that she may not have any light left in her. Her light is depressed and fading. This is what happens to Amaterasu: she forgets who she truly is, just like you did when you became a wallflower.

**Everything is dying**

Something needs to be done. If Amaterasu remains in her cave, the world will die. Nothing can grow and, in time, everyone and everything will slowly starve to death. There will be no nature, no food, no way of sustaining life and, finally, the earth will die a long, slow death.

So, in the story, the myriad gods come together and seek a way to get Amaterasu out of the cave. You may want to put yourself in the place of the gods with this enormously delicate task. What is going to persuade Amaterasu to come out of the cave? In other words, what is going to get **you** out - or the bit of you that knows and believes that **you could come out?** The gods are going to have to devise a really, really brilliant way to get Amaterasu out. She cannot be forced. If she is to come out, she needs to come out of her own free will. Maybe you know how this feels - you have struggled to come out of your cave for years, and most of your attempts have driven you back even deeper into the cave. This is the dilemma that the myriad gods face.

This story is a metaphor and mirrors your own journey out of the cave, when you, too, can step into the sunlight and take your place in the world.

### Exercise: How do the myriad gods get Amaterasu out of the cave?

How do the gods persuade Amaterasu to come out of the cave? I invite you now to imagine you are the myriad gods: what strategy would you come up with to get her out of the cave? This is an exercise I offer in one of my courses. Imagine how desperate the gods must be and how much depends on them being successful. Put yourself in their shoes. Then write down all the things the gods do to get Amaterasu out. Be bold, be expansive – remember you are a god with a god's powers and imagination.

Refrain from the temptation to look at the next section, in which you will discover what the gods actually do. Your answers will provide valuable clues into your own mindset and provide insights to assist you in your own process of coming out of your cave. This is another way of communicating directly with your unconscious.

When you have discovered in the next section, how the myriad gods indeed get Amaterasu out, you may want to reflect back on your answers here.

## Coming out into the light

*This is what the gods actually do in the myth, to persuade Amaterasu to come out of the cave:*

So at last it happens, the Big Event. The myriad gods come together and create a magnificent celebration for Amaterasu - a strategy that they believe will inevitably bring Amaterasu out of the cave. They are aware that Amaterasu has forgotten she's the Sun Goddess and she's been so long in that cave that she's forgotten about the Light that is shining within her. She's forgotten what it's like to shine her light on the world.

When she hears the sound of cocks crowing outside her cave, Amaterasu starts to get curious. She remembers that the cocks only crow when the dawn has come; indeed, the cocks only crow when she's beginning to shine her light on the earth. Intrigued, she draws a little closer to the mouth of the cave. As she does this she is aware of a lot of activity outside. She can hear whispering, and many other strange and perplexing noises. Then she hears the more familiar sounds of construction; she wonders what on earth can be going on out there?

Then she hears music - music that she knows only too well. It's none other than the music of Uzume, the dawn goddess. She can hear the dawn goddess's cries of joy as she dances her wild dance and she's reminded that Uzume only dances like that when the dawn is coming. When she hears the gods laughing and cheering, her curiosity has no bounds. She calls out to them, "What's happening out there?" Since it's the first time she has heard her own voice for a very long time, and her voice probably sounds weak.

The gods answer back, "A new sun goddess has arrived, who is even more powerful!"

Amaterasu wonders what they can mean. Who can this new sun goddess possibly be? She peeps out.

*As soon as she does so, she sees her own reflection in the giant mirror that is facing the mouth of the cave and is pointed towards her. In the mirror she sees her own Light reflected, which is even stronger than it was before. During her time in the cave she has been through many things; she has suffered inside the cave and she has found depths within herself that she never knew were there. She sees wisdom in her eyes as they shine back from the mirror and she feels an even deeper desire to shine her Light. She takes another step forward and* **she is out.**

*That moment is quite unlike any other she has experienced. She rediscovers how wonderful it is to be out. When she looks down and sees the terrible state that the world is in, as a result of her absence - compassion moves in her. Then she sees the other things the gods have been preparing for her - the magical objects that line the pathway to her Sacred Weaving Hall and the new palace that has been built for her. The myriad gods then adorn her with new jewellery and fresh garments, even more magnificent than before. When she steps back into her Sacred Weaving Hall she finds her handmaids waiting for her, and she realises how much she's missed being with them and serving her purpose in the world.*

*So, she sends her rays out to shine on her people and, as she does so, her world begins to get bigger and brighter. She feels joy in her heart as she sees the joy of the gods and her people, as her Light floods back to the world. Then, when she sees all is well in the world, Amaterasu returns to her handmaids and together they continue to weave the Fabric of the Universe, creating new landscapes, new horizons and new universes, repairing whatever has crumbled or disintegrated - or releasing it into the flow of nature, allowing the process of death and decay to do its work. Amaterasu speeds this up, and all the insects, birds and animals that are sustained by this can flourish more fully.*

If you were participating in one of my courses, you would have had an opportunity to enact this, or a similar story, in collaboration with other people, and explore Amaterasu's emergence from the cave. This is often a moving, joyful and inspiring experience, as it mirrors your own entrapment and re-emergence from the cave.

## Rena

*Rena felt constricted in her everyday life - she felt as if she was living in a straightjacket. Her job in marketing was taxing and gradually she had become more depressed and more aware of her shortcomings. Unable to snap out of her depression, she had retreated more and more into her shell.*

*When Rena played Amaterasu coming out of the cave, a part of her woke up and came alive. Watching her was like seeing someone light a taper - as if everyone had switched on the lights within her. As she went through the course, more and more of her came out, and she saw how she had shut herself down, through taking everything too seriously.*

*She walked into work as a totally new person and her work colleagues were struck by the difference in her. She was no longer depressed. Having felt this part of her come alive, Rena knew she needed to keep working on this on an ongoing basis, or she would shut down again, and her old habits would return. She signed up for my improvisation course and, in this, discovered what a dynamo she truly was. More and more of her dynamic self began to emerge, as she gave herself permission to express more of this and to trust more in her instincts. A very different Rena began to emerge.*

## Exercise: It's your turn to shine

So now you will have an opportunity to recreate this experience for yourself in Audio 3 of Bonus 4. You will be able to focus on aspects of this story that are most pertinent to you, exploring those barriers gently and honouring your own deeper choices. In this you will be preparing the way for your own emergence into the sunlight - creating the potential for new neuronal pathways and a new way of being in the world.

If you have already participated in one of my groups, this process may reawaken the experience you had in the group, and thus enable you to go far deeper with it and derive even further benefits.

## New patterns

Participants regularly write to me, often years afterwards, telling me of the many ways they have been able to come out of the shadows and move into the sunlight, as a result of the Sunflower Effect. They have created a new pattern and new neuronal pathways for manifesting a different way of being in the world.

They report the things they have achieved, which would never have been possible without the support of the group and the process. They retain the memory of their experience and say they have never forgotten the transformative experiences they have had, which they can recall and reactivate at any time. Nor, can they forget the group of people they did this with, who supported them through the challenges and helped them overcome their doubts and fears - and to step into a new future. Now all they need to do to step into that future and live their life from this place.

We are getting close to the end of the journey from wallflower to sunflower, although, in some ways, this journey does not have an end because, as in life, we are continually moving through the stages of this journey. This is what will enable you to make deep change. In the final chapter, I will be offering you some extra tools and guidance that will help you to make long-lasting change - so you can truly live your life as a sunflower.

## Chapter 10

# Living Your Life as a Sunflower

**Tools and resources that will support you continuing on the path to becoming the person you've always dreamed of being**

How does a wallflower truly become a sunflower? The sunflower part of you is already written into you: it's already there. It's just deeply buried away, as I have been describing in the first nine chapters of this book. The Sunflower Effect is a symbolic way in which you can move into the sunshine and out of your dark hiding place. You have been discovering this and exploring this (if you've been participating in the exercises) and you may be aware of the internal shifts you have already made which are going to pave the way to a much bigger transition.

In this chapter, I will be giving you a blueprint by which you can chart your progress from wallflower to sunflower, which you can come back to again and again. This will help you to remind yourself of where you've come from, what it's taken to get where you are now - and the journey that may still lie ahead.

## The stages of the journey

In observing my own progress and in supporting my clients to become their sunflower - the person that they've always wanted to be - I have identified a number of distinct stages. Awareness of these will, I hope, save you some heartache and help you to progress much faster.

PLEASE NOTE: Be aware that like the Sunflower Effect process, these stages are not necessarily linear and you may find yourself moving back and forwards at any time in the journey, as I will be explaining in Stage 4 – Zigzag Progress. There is no right and wrong way of doing the journey.

**Stage 1: Taking the first step**

Without doubt the hardest stage of the journey is to get started. If you've picked up this book you have started. If you did the commitment exercise, you have started. If you've already made some attempts to change yourself, even if you think that those attempts have "failed" - then you have started. Acknowledge yourself for that. Right now you may just want a little change to your life. That's how I started; I was fed up of being a wallflower and I had no idea what lay in store for me. All I needed to do was to take the first step. And then, when I discovered how much better my life was after taking the first step, and indeed how easy it had been - I was encouraged to take another step.

It's so much easier to simply bemoan your misfortune and all that is painful in being a wallflower. You can entertain yourself for years doing this, as I did, justifying why you're not living the life you want to live. But when you are doing this, you are literally poisoning your mind with toxic thoughts that will make it harder for you to move forward. Some of the tools in this chapter, along with other exercises in the book, will help you shift out of this negative mindset.

But when you take the first step on the path and commit to the journey - and find a way to experience **safety, support and stretching** as described in this book - you take a giant leap for your life. It does not matter that you don't yet have full trust or self-belief, or you still have some doubts that the process will work for you. All you need to do is to stick with it. You may feel that there is a very big gap between where you are now and where you want to be. You may wish that you didn't have to face your fear of falling. You will need support to move through your fear – with support it will be relatively easy. This is why the most important transformational aspects of the Sunflower Effect are achieved through face-to-face interaction in a safe and supportive group with other people who have had similar experiences.

When you feel secure enough in yourself and feel some confidence growing in you, it will be time to move to the second stage.

### Stage 2: Creating the new pattern

The second stage is the creation of the new pattern, the new neuronal pathways, which I have described in this book. All nine elements of the Sunflower Effect help to forge this new pattern. As I have explained, your unconscious knows no difference between what you're doing in an imaginary situation, and when you're doing something amazing for real in your outside life. Your imagination is a powerful transformational machine that works through your unconscious. And it lives inside your own head.

When you act out a story - or play out a symbolic action, as in Amaterasu emerging from the cave - you are drawing on similar tools. This is what Sue Jennings has called "a rehearsal for life," in which you are laying the foundations for what can potentially happen in the outside world. Every person will experience the story in a different way - because each one of us has a different story, even when we share similar stories with other people.

Through this, you will be expressing all the different parts of your multi-faceted self: the darker parts; the lighter parts; the joyful parts; the frightened parts; the inhuman parts and the monstrous parts. At the same time, you will be working through the layers of unconscious barriers that have been keeping you a wallflower. You may need multiple opportunities to do this, so as to forge the new pattern over a period of time - because this pattern does need time to take effect. (It varies with each individual, but most people notice a significant shift after 3 months.) This is what builds trust in yourself. Trust is the glue that holds the new pattern together. When others who have made a commitment to achieve a breakthrough with you witness you, this will further intensify the effectiveness of the process: for all the reasons I have described in Witnessing (Chapter 6).

The only really important thing to do at this stage is to stick with it. Resistance will come up; self-doubt will come up; distractions will come up. All you need to do is to commit to the journey and you will get through this.

## Stage 3: The rehearsal becomes real life

The next stage is taking the rehearsal into the outside world. It's very powerful to take your discoveries beyond being something that's in your head or imagination, into your day-to-day experience. When you go and repeat the pattern in real life, since you have already created a pattern, **it's easier for this pattern to repeat itself over and over again.**

This process happens naturally through the Sunflower Effect. You can also consciously create it as a result of doing one of the exercises in the last 2 chapters. Strongly imagine yourself as Amaterasu when you want to be more visible. Feel this throughout your body. Start with walking or moving as Amaterasu and notice the impact that this has on you. You might then find the courage to speak as Amaterasu and see how other people respond to you. If you want to feel more powerful you may want to imagine yourself as Susanno or the myriad gods.

Your unconscious responds to emotions, it responds to how you feel - and this is what links your conscious and unconscious mind together and opens up a portal of communication between them. When you naturally start acting confidently in the outside world, your conscious mind will register your experience as real and will record this as a memory - and evidence that you really are making headway. This is when you will start seeing shifts in your mindset, which will translate into **ultimate proof**.

When I started doing things that I never thought I would do, I knew I had ultimate proof. The experiences that I was having, and the people I was meeting, meant I was living a life that I had never dared to dream. Each one of my experiences was a total miracle, and it was immensely exciting and fulfilling. I started to broaden my horizons and as I did this, I expanded even more.

Clients are surprised when they tell me that something happened in their outside life that was almost an exact repeat of what they did in one of our sessions. When you start doing some of the things that take you away from the sidelines and make you believe that you're a sunflower out in the world shining your light, then you know you have the building blocks of lasting confidence. This might be speaking up in front of groups; enjoying social situations; laughing more; having more fun; achieving small things. It might mean achieving much bigger things and really surprising yourself and everybody else.

Eventually you will start manifesting these same experiences in the world on a regular basis. Instead of others criticizing you and undermining your confidence, they will start praising you, applauding you, thanking you and valuing you. Each time that happens, your comfort zone expands just a little bit more, so you can, in time, shed your identity as a wallflower - and take that courageous step away from the sidelines into discovering you truly **are** a sunflower.

Celebrate each achievement. The more you celebrate your progress, the deeper the impact this will make on your unconscious, and the more your unconscious will collaborate with you to create even deeper successes.

## Stage 4: Zigzag Progress

Before you build the kind of confidence that really is going to make a permanent difference to your life, you will also need to prepared for the roller coaster ride that lies ahead. Therefore, a crucial stage of the journey from wallflower to sunflower is to **expect Zigzag Progress.**

We actually don't grow/make progress in a straight line; we grow in a zigzag pattern. This how all things grow; even plants don't grow consistently, they grow in little spurts. If you are a parent, you may have noticed the haphazard growth of your children at certain times. This seems to be one of the irrefutable laws of nature; even financial markets reflect this pattern.

Yet almost all humans seem to believe that, when it comes to their own progress, they should only make steady improvements. As soon as they hit upon even a small setback, they take this as evidence that they have failed. This is the power of our negative mind, fuelled by the Resistor and influenced by the competitive culture in which we live, which praises winners and shames all others.

When it comes to any kind of personal development work, sometimes we move forwards and sometimes we move back. We may take a spurt forward as a result of making a significant breakthrough, and other times we get really stuck or encounter obstacles. This is all part of integrating your new behaviour in your life - and moving from wallflower to sunflower is a big shift in your *modus operandi*.

This was a steep learning curve for me. I spent a lot of time despairing about whether or not I would ever crawl out the hole I inevitably found myself falling back into. I wish someone had told me about Zigzag Progress, so I would have been more patient and understanding of my process. I slowed down my progress hugely though the harsh criticisms coming from my negative mind.

At times it's important to process the experiences you have had, particularly experiences that have challenged your *modus operandi*. Let yourself go through this with grace and ease. Take a break and do some of the things you enjoy. But, also, don't stay away too long or you're going to block your future progress. It's a bit like if you fall off a horse, you have to get back into the saddle. Generally, the sooner you get back on track the better. That's why it's really important to have ongoing support.

## Stage 5: The power of major setbacks

There will be times when you will hit a major setback: a major obstacle; or a deeper level of stuckness may surface seemingly from nowhere; or you'll have a very destructive experience that totally wipes you out. It may take all your confidence away so you'll feel as if you're back in that same place you were in years ago. You may remember, as I described in my journey, when I almost had a nervous breakdown. I lost all confidence and fell into a very deep, dark place. It was soul-destroying. This is a really good moment to seek help - to do a course or workshop, or to reach out to a professional that you trust. It's most important to take some action at this time.

Welcome (if you can) such setbacks when they come, because they will strengthen you and prepare you for what is to come - the bigger challenges that are going to enable you to build a cast-iron confidence, the long-lasting confidence that will in time become a natural part of you.

Major setbacks are extremely valuable. This is how every sunflower came to their fullest and deepest potential. They received encouragement and support from those around them. Those who were supporting them believed in them and saw the potential sunflower in them. They had setbacks but they got through those setbacks - either through their own initiatives or with help from a variety of sources. Often, just the person they needed to help them get-through the setback turned up just when they needed them. A little further on, they began to see some indication of the progress they were making when people, who didn't know them, and had no vested interest in giving praise for praise's sake, were acknowledging them. This kind of praise really counts for something, as every budding sunflower knows. They are commanding more respect and, as result, they will naturally begin to expand even more.

When you get through a setback, you will know that you can trust yourself to take bigger risks and to stretch in bigger ways, trusting more in your ability to get through. Most of the risks you now take will work out: some still won't - but they will become powerful learning experiences through which your sunflower will develop stronger foundations.

## Stage 6: Keep going no matter what

Keep on broadening your horizons. Keep on expanding all the things that we've talked about in stages 1, 2 and 3; just practice, practice, practice. You might set yourself small challenges. You might set yourself a whole list of things that you'd really love to be doing and then do those one by one.

*Touching the Void* is a film based on a true story of how a climber with a broken leg managed to inch his way, bit by bit, from the crevasse that he had fallen into, to reach base camp where his fellow climber was waiting - a huge distance, particularly for someone with severe injuries. When Simpson started the journey, he didn't believe he could get to base camp. He, however, discovered he could move himself a tiny bit and this was better than lying there and freezing to death. So he just kept on inching himself forward. How he found his way to base camp was an incredible feat, but some survival instinct in him led him there. He arrived only in the nick of time before his companion was about to pack up camp.

This same survival instinct lives in you. It's how you have got through your life and survived your biggest setbacks and ordeals. This is why the Sunflower Effect teaches you to access and operate more from your intuitive side - because this is going to fast track your progress. You don't have to believe you can do it; you just have to take one step, then another, then the next one. This is how eventually you will develop into a fully blossomed sunflower.

## Stage 7: It really does get easier and easier

After a while, you will need to expend much less effort on expanding, because you can rely on your skills, your reputation and your capacity to attract others to help you to achieve your goals. For the same effort you can achieve ten times what you achieved when you started out. It just gets easier and easier. This is when you know you are making real progress, and your sunflower is drinking in the sunlight and all the nutrients that are sustaining your progress. Your life is flowing and unfolding in delightful ways - as described in Out of Your Head in Chapter 6.

This is the pathway by which the seeding sunflower becomes a fully-grown sunflower. The tallest known sunflower grew to 9.17 m (30 ft 1 in), which is simply enormous for a flowering plant; it's the height of a tree. To expand to your fullest potential as a sunflower, repeat the previous stages that I have described, until you have reached your fullest expansion. This may be a lifetime's journey. The sky's the limit to what you can achieve. Never stop growing. This is what will keep you feeling young, vital and alive, no matter what age you are.

## Some useful tools

What follows is a series of tools to sustain you on your journey. You may find them helpful, particularly during those times when you hit a roadblock or you need some extra support.

### The power of acknowledgment

Acknowledgement is empowering. Get good at receiving appreciation, acknowledgment, applause, compliments and recognition from others. If anybody acknowledges you, resist the temptation to deny it or belittle it. Instead, simply say "thank you". Enjoy the acknowledgment. In doing so, you are not becoming too big for your boots; you are merely accepting their acknowledgement with grace. You are acknowledging the gift they are offering you, and their own qualities that they see reflected in you.

Remember, too, that every time you acknowledge and see the beauty and strengths in another person, you acknowledge and empower yourself. You step into a bigger part of yourself - and the potential that lies within you. When a giant recognises another giant, or an equal recognises another equal - each one expands.

You achieve this most when you "hold your own shape," a term I first heard from a friend of mine, David de Vall. By this he means that you are not disappearing, making yourself smaller or giving your power away so that another person will feel more comfortable in relation to you. You are holding your ground, your boundaries and maintaining your psychological shape. A simple way to do this is to send your energy into the ground. Be aware of your body and the physical space you are occupying. This will also bring you present and make you appear more confident.

Any time you find that other people are not acknowledging you, you can always acknowledge yourself. You can go and stand in front of the YouTube applause video that you will find on the fromwallflowertosunflower.com website and receive that applause. This is a very powerful and instant confidence-building system. If you find that going to a website, or picking up this book, actually reminds you of who you really are - I suggest you do that often.

## A success diary

I suggest you keep a diary of your successes. Every evening note anything that you have done in the day that has been positive - even small things. If there was something that was really positive, I want you to give yourself a big acknowledgment. You might want to imagine all your friends are really, really pleased that you've achieved that thing and are celebrating with you in the way you like to celebrate best.

It's very important if you have a big success that you acknowledge it in a significant way. Give yourself a little holiday; give yourself a little break; buy yourself some flowers or some new shoes; or some little treat - as an acknowledgement of what you've accomplished. An actor I knew told me how he always gave himself a treat after he'd done an audition – often it was just buying himself a coffee. Whilst he was drinking the coffee he praised himself for doing the audition, even if he thought he hadn't got the part. Not surprisingly, he was one of the more successful actors I knew.

**The power of small steps**

Keep taking small steps. Like the race between the hare and the tortoise, the tortoise gets to the finishing line first, because he keeps taking small, slow steps.

**18 behaviours you need to avoid if you're serious about becoming a fully blossomed sunflower**

This brings us to the eighteen behaviours, which are hampering your progress. If you are serious about becoming a fully blossomed sunflower, these are deep-rooted habits that it would be good to avoid, a bit like you avoid dog shit on the pavement.

Notice which ones you particularly do. This is not about blaming or judging yourself, nor feeling bad about any way you are sabotaging yourself. It's just good to be alert to every time you find yourself doing them, so that you can gradually start eliminating them. This could be through simply observing the behaviour and making another behaviour choice. You will also find many useful tools in this chapter and the rest of this book to assist you, along with your own resources and copious advice from countless sources: books, magazines, the Internet, friends, people you meet etc.

1. Criticising yourself.
2. Seeing yourself as a wallflower.
3. Saying should, must, can't or try. (Try instead saying choose to, want to, love to.)
4. Comparing yourself to other people, particularly comparing yourself negatively to others.
5. Doubting yourself.
6. Isolating yourself.
7. Seeing yourself as a failure.
8. Punishing yourself for things that happened in the past.
9. Blaming other people.
10. Believing in the helpful opinions and advice of other people who don't understand what it's like to be a wallflower.
11. Compromising and putting up with things.
12. Being a perfectionist, and believing you have to get it right, or that "it has to be perfect".
13. Saying yes when you want to say no.
14. Waiting politely for other people to speak first.
15. Keeping quiet.
16. Believing you can do it on your own.
17. Waiting for the perfect time and conditions to get started
18. Changing direction every time you hit an obstacle.

Some of these habits, however, are not easy to remove and will require deeper work. Do the work that is necessary to free yourself from them. If you notice that you are beating yourself up about these behaviours, this is not the purpose of this exercise. This is another opportunity to practice self-compassion. Think of yourself as a scientist working on a very important experiment. A scientist sees every so- called "failed experiment" as a negative test result – and a stepping-stone towards their ultimate goal. Often the negative test results lead to even more important discoveries.

## The power of naming

The names and labels you give yourself hold a powerful magic. What names do you call yourself, especially the ones you use inside your own head: wallflower, pathetic person, loser, fool or idiot? Catch yourself out every time you call yourself one of these names so they don't become part of your identity. This is what happens to most people, and why they may struggle to make any progress. Whatever negative names you have ever called yourself (even in jest), it's time to say goodbye to those names. Leave them behind in Amaterasu's cave, or write the name on pieces of paper and burn them or bury them in the ground. It's time to let them go. There's no shame in those names or of being in the cave. But after letting them go, when you come out and step into the light, you will shine even brighter.

Start right now by calling yourself a sunflower, a confident person – or however you want to name yourself or be seen by others. Write down these new names in your notebook. Claim these new names. Do this often and watch your confidence soar.

## The elastic band exercise

This exercise is a very effective way of breaking the power of the critical voice over you. You can do this very simply, and nobody will know what you are doing. The only thing you need is an elastic band. You might want to choose an attractive elastic band, but any old elastic band will do. If you're a woman you might have a stretchy bracelet that's easy to take on and off.

So you put the elastic band onto one of your wrists and then, whenever you notice that a critical thought slips into your mind - "I shouldn't have done that"; "I'm so stupid for saying that"; "I'm not good at that"; "I've messed it up again" - simply remove the elastic band from one wrist and put it on the other wrist. That's all you need to do. But as you do that, you note that it's time to let go of that thought and to switch off any further activity of the critical voice.

When it comes back you repeat the process, which will serve as a reminder to yourself to reduce or diffuse the number of negative thoughts you entertain. Gradually you will need to switch the elastic band between your wrists much less frequently. This is the purpose of the exercise. If you forget to do it for a while, that's OK. Forgive yourself and return to the practice.

**Transforming the critical voice**

At times your negative thoughts can be really useful. They may remind you of something that you are doing that you want to change. So maybe you can say: "OK Critical Voice, let's see if I can find another way of saying that, that's easier for me to get along with, and that's more motivating."

So instead of saying "I'm not very good at that," you might say: "This is still something that I want to work on, and that I'd like to get better at, so I'll sign up for that course, ask X to mentor me, join that group or organisation... etc." Thus you replace the self-criticism with a more constructive thought and, maybe, an action step that will take you closer to where you want to be.

This is an exercise in awareness, and a positive way of transforming and using that old habit of self-consciousness. In other words, of being aware of what you are doing to yourself through your thoughts. Through this, you will begin to change the course that you are on. Instead of sailing off to self-consciousness or shyness or any of those other states that are uncomfortable, you are gently changing your course through self-awareness - so that you can make another choice (maybe though some of the exercises I have described in this book). Do you want to sail to self-confidence and the life of a sunflower, or do you want to move back to being stuck on the sidelines?

Many of my clients practice mindfulness as a way of supporting themselves to maintain the progress they have made in my courses. This is another way of achieving self-awareness, and there are many resources available on the Internet.

## Dealing with "helpful" people who don't understand how difficult it is to move from wallflower to sunflower

Helpful people who advise you to do all the things that you know you should do but can't, can be deeply disempowering. They don't realise it, but they're getting a kick from handing out this unasked-for advice, and they are also easily offended if you reject it.

Say, "Thank you for your advice, I'll consider that," and smile. Then walk away, or make it clear that you are not inviting further advice from them. If the person persists, you may need to say: *"You know that's exactly what lots of other people have told me. I'm well aware of this and wish I could do exactly as you say. I know you meant to be helpful, so what you can do that would be more supportive to me is.."* And then you tell them whatever they can do to help you. Some of the tools in this book may give you some ideas of how other people can help you.

One of the things that I ask people to do is to acknowledge any small positive changes they see in me. Or I will tell them that I am on a pathway to doing something about this, and I ask them if they will be on my side. Just knowing that they are supporting me on my journey makes an enormous difference and we both come out of the situation feeling positive, instead one of us feeling uncomfortable.

## Twenty behaviours that sunflowers automatically do

Below are twenty behaviours that sunflowers naturally do, often without even thinking about it. When you notice you are doing more of these things, you will know that you have truly begun to enter the place of the sunflower and, inevitably, the behaviours that block your progress, which I described earlier, will simply slip away.

1. You know that you are OK. Not just that - you know that you are OK **just the way you are.**

2. You are compassionate to yourself.

3. You listen to your instincts and gut impulses.

4. You realise that there is no such thing as failure.

5. You speak up when you feel the impulse to speak, particularly when you feel this from your gut instincts.

6. You seek help when you need it. You find mentors everywhere in your life. You find people who are like you, or who are kindred spirits with whom you can give and receive support.

7. You see beauty in the world. You practice gratitude for all that is positive in your world, especially the small things.

8. As a sunflower you know what you are good at and what your strengths are.

9. You live life lightly.

10. You trust yourself.

11. You find new ways of stretching your comfort zone.

12. You never stop learning and growing.
13. You celebrate your successes and you reward yourself whenever you achieve something, however small.
14. You keep going. You "get back on the horse as soon as you've fallen off it," or as soon as you possibly can.
15. You learn from the feedback you receive from others.
16. You take time out to have fun, and you make a play an important part of your life. You're always looking for ways you can play, especially when life gets tough or too serious.
17. You acknowledge yourself, even for the tiny little things that you do.
18. You see the positive qualities in others. And when you see the positive qualities in others you also see these positive qualities in yourself. You could not see them in another person unless they were also in yourself in some way. This is known as the Mirror Principle.
19. You're continuously breaking patterns. When you see a new pattern forming that is not very helpful to you, then, unless you particularly want to keep that pattern, you take the necessary steps to break it.
20. When you feel like nothing is happening, you are aware that often you are on the edge of making your biggest breakthrough.

Praise yourself internally each time you notice that you are doing these behaviours, and know that you are well on your way to becoming a fully blossomed sunflower. When these behaviours become second nature, then you will notice that your life will begin to flow in delightful ways. You will worry less; have more fun; solutions will effortlessly arrive to your most intractable problems; and you will experience more joy in your life. Even your biggest challenges will hold less fear for you because you know you can meet those challenges in your own way.

## Reflection

We're now reaching the end of this book and this is an opportunity for you to review where you have been and what you have learned. What insights and revelations have come to you as you've been reading, even the ones you don't dare to name in case you get them wrong. Jot them down in your notebook. Has anything significant happened whilst you have been reading this book that seems relevant? Jot this down too.

## Commitment

Cast your mind back to the commitment you made in the very first chapter. You may remember back to that process and you may actually want to return to that commitment right now and see where you are with it. Are you still strong in your commitment? This commitment will take you far beyond the confines of this book and I suggest you look at it regularly. You may choose to revisit the video in Bonus 1 and have that commitment witnessed over again.

## Wallflowers

Remember the chapter about the perks of being a wallflower? What is a wallflower really? Can you remember some these really positive things that people said about wallflowers?

*A wallflower is the most beautiful person you can meet but very few people see that.*

*A wallflower observes and knows things about people that no one else would know.*

*A wallflower is probably one of the most interesting people that I've ever met.*

So remember what a wallflower really is. Reframe your experience of being a wallflower. Claim the positive aspects of being a wallflower that are true for you. You will never lose them.

## Resources

What are the resources that you've acquired during your time on the sidelines, or in your cave, or in whatever place you feel you've retreated to? During the course of this book you may have identified something you need to let go of. You may need some support to truly let go of it (does anyone come to mind who could help you?), or you may simply be able to let go of it right now.

Remember the Amaterasu exercise (Audio 1 of Bonus 4) and finding your inner sunflower: that light, that radiance that lives inside of you and which is your birthright. Remember all the things that a sunflower does. A sunflower is not somebody who is so full of themselves that they only see themselves. A sunflower looks around the world and sees the beauty in it. A true sunflower is a worker, a doer. A sunflower serves.

Remember that, in nature, the sunflower plant produces oil that has multiple nutritional and healing properties. It has powerful environmental effects that will remove toxins. When you focus on your potential to become a sunflower, you, too, call forward your own power to detoxify yourself of negativity.

For most sunflowers, it's the experience of contributing to the world around us that makes the most difference. To contribute is to give, to offer, and **giving is in the nature of being human.** When you give, you feel good, because you have something valuable to offer. This could be sharing the gifts, insights and wisdom within you; speaking up at a meeting; or standing up for something that you believe in. This is what brings long-lasting fulfilment and satisfaction for most people. Often sunflowers serve best by just being themselves, by shining their light and bringing a little more brightness into the world.

When you claim yourself as a sunflower you claim all this. Claim it now. Take a moment to stop and envision the person you are becoming. See yourself as you truly want or dream to be. In time you will become this person. Breathe your future self into your solar plexus. BE IT.

## Daring to dream

This potential lives in you and is seeking to be expressed in your life, and it doesn't matter how old you are when you get started. It just takes a very small amount of courage to set the process in motion.

**PERSONAL NOTE:** Most of the time that I was on my journey from wallflower to sunflower, I didn't know what I was doing. I was in the dark and had no real idea of where I was going. I didn't have any sense of my destiny because I didn't have the confidence or self-esteem to dare to dream of anything much.

However, deep inside me I knew that my life had a deeper purpose. I felt that I was not alive just to go through the motions of what everyone else does because that's what you're supposed to do. I found a different path. In fact I missed out on some of the stages that most people go through in their lives, because that wasn't my path. The seed that had been planted within me, way back, just kept on growing. And it kept on nudging me to keep going, and then I did start to dream. It didn't matter that many of those dreams were not the dreams I eventually fulfilled. A much bigger dream and destiny was waiting for me. One that I didn't know existed.

All those "other" dreams were dreams of my ego, the dreams of becoming a successful actor and playwright. Neither of these would have brought the kind of fulfilment I experience in my life now, which has brought me to writing this book. They would have felt great for a time, but I predict that they would have felt empty and hollow after a while. I was seeking something different from what I see in the most successful and inspired playwrights and actors.

Right now you may not have an inkling of the potential that lives in you. You just are holding the seed of what you could be. It's a twinkle in your eye, just as a child is a twinkle in their parents' eyes before they come into the world.

**Your Secret Weapon**

Remember your Secret Weapon and finding a way of channelling Susanno, the storm god's energy. This is very empowering. We all have negative aspects of ourselves; we all have emotions that need releasing, freeing and channelling. From time to time, remembering Susanno and finding Susanno within you can be deeply freeing.

In time Susanno discovers a positive expression for his destructive energy. The story continues that he uses this energy to slay a powerful dragon. He brings back the sword he finds within the dragon's belly, and offers it to Amaterasu in acknowledgment: of who she is; the light she bears; and the important work she is doing.

Susanno gives up competitiveness, chaos and destructiveness in place of humility, acknowledgement and grace – and as a result he becomes truly divine. He steps into his godhead and his full maturity. He heals the rift between himself and Amaterasu, so they both have greater respect for each other.

This is the same as healing the rifts within yourself. Through this you will achieve inner wholeness, and this will strengthen your confidence and enable you to reach your full potential and maturity.

## Power of the imagination

Your imagination is powerful, as I hope you have learned through reading this book. You can tell this, too, because some people are able to create powerful physical effects through the power of their imagination: a phantom pregnancy; anxiety states; psychosomatic illnesses etc. This is how negatively powerful your imagination can be, if you let it. These effects are produced either unconsciously or automatically in the cortex of the brain.

The imagination can equally create positive effects, when the imagination is used consciously for positive outcomes. All successful people know this and they use tools that call in the power of the imagination to create multi-million businesses, launch products, build careers and change the world. This is what you are drawing on when you do the exercises in this book, or use the tools I have suggested here. Eventually you will start manifesting these same experiences in the world. Instead of others criticising you and undermining your confidence, they will start praising you, applauding you, thanking you and valuing you. Then you know you are truly on your way to becoming a fully blossomed sunflower.

## Vulnerability is your true strength

Vulnerability is your true strength. Those who exhibit no vulnerability are not really strong – often because they are denying their tender, human parts, their vulnerability. So they are building a false strength, a rigid strength that isn't real strength. A rigid strength will break very easily when something hits it. A very powerful building will literally crumble if it relies on rigid strength to keep it standing. In areas where there are earthquakes, buildings are built out of different materials, materials that will allow movement. True strength is when there is room for flexibility, and for the ups and downs of life.

Thus the person who has this kind of rigid I-can't–show–any- weakness strength often breaks when they encounter real adversity. They lose their job, or their business goes bankrupt, they lose a lot of money or a key person in their life - and they do in fact break. Their false self-image literally shatters into pieces and they don't know who they are any more. This can lead to severe psychological breakdown because their system just can't handle that degree of shock and trauma.

In fact our whole system is vulnerable. Our psychological system can only withstand so much. That's why we became wallflowers - because that's a way of protecting us psychologically. We actually need to thank our system for doing that because we're still here – we survived. If you ignore this, you are heading for a cropper.

You may remember my account of my near breakdown during my acting days when I was so motivated by a desire to be successful that I was unaware of my limitations as a human being. During my wallflower days I had had no hope of being successful but, once I discovered it, I was going for it 200%. I had no awareness of the psychological limits of my own wellbeing – and the director of the play I was in, was unaware that he was playing with fire. He pushed me to the limit and I was in a very bad way for a very long time. It took an enormous amount of time to undo the damage of a few weeks. However although I was angry with the director for taking advantage of my willingness to go for it, even he admitted he was amazed when I kept on going. So I learned that I couldn't make other people responsible for my wellbeing. I have to take care of it myself, and this was one of the most powerful lessons I learned in my life.

Vulnerability is powerful because it connects you with other people. Many inspirational speakers talk about the experiences they have had in their lives because it makes them more human. The TED speakers do this superbly. Watch any TED talk and the speaker will often be recounting painful experiences they had in their life which changed the course of their lives and woke them up to a new discovery (and this can lead to a ground breaking scientific breakthrough) or opened up a new path in their lives which subsequently enabled them to fulfil their potential. This makes them just like you. You can see they have fears and challenges too, and you learn through them how to overcome your own challenges. Thus, through the work of Brené Brown and other authors/speakers, vulnerability (often confused with weakness) is gradually becoming more acceptable.

This is one of the reasons that the Sunflower Effect is so effective - because it gives a safe context in which wallflowers can be vulnerable. They can be open and honest about their experiences so that they can move forward and put those experiences behind them.

### The cave as a resource

When Amaterasu emerges from her cave, she is curious because the gods have announced that a new and even more powerful sun goddess has arrived. She discovers that goddess is none other than herself.

Remember the cave is also a **safe place**, a place of resource that you can return to at any time. Every time you move back into the cave and come out again, you will be even more powerful than you were before. You are on a journey in which you will start to spend more time out of the cave than in the cave. But it's always fine to go back in that cave - you need to retreat from time to time. Everybody does. Overcoming adversity and setbacks makes you stronger. This is what makes Amaterasu more powerful; they will strengthen you too at a fundamental level. Sometimes it won't feel like it, but tell yourself that this is happening and you'll gradually begin to feel the positive pleasure of it so that you can step into your expanded potential. It doesn't matter if you don't feel it yet; this will come in time. Trust it will come.

**Saying goodbye**

So now it's time to say "goodbye". This is always a poignant moment for me when I'm working with a group. I look round at the sea of faces who have been with me for 12 or more weeks. I see their shining eyes and the progress that each one of them has made during the course of us working together.

Obviously I can't see the progress that you've made unless you actually write to me and tell me about it. (You can write to me though the book website and tell me about anything that's been positive for you though reading this book.) But I'm imagining right now that I'm looking round at you, along with all the other people that have read, or are still to read, this book. I'm looking at your face and I'm also seeing the changes that I know that you will make if you keep walking this path, if you truly claim yourself as a sunflower and start living your life as a sunflower.

This is what one courageous man wrote to me, who had travelled 200 miles, once a week for 12 weeks, to face his fears and finally triumph over them. His account is as much a message to you, which is why I am including it here.

## Stefan

*I had been suffering from social anxiety from a very young age. I had tried CBT, anger management therapy, hypnotherapy, past life regression therapy and went to see many psychologists but, the fact was, that none of them helped to reduce my anxiety. All I gained is an understanding of where my anxiety stems from and what causes it. In fact I would feel even more sad and disappointed at the end because I knew it had failed - and also because of the huge amount of money I had to pay for these courses.*

*I was very determined to cure my anxiety so I was always looking for new ways and kept hoping that something might help. In my searches online, I came across someone who had managed to overcome his social anxiety. He said that the most efficient and only way to overcome social anxiety is to join a group, which allows its members to start expressing themselves and face their fears in a safe and supportive environment. This is why I decided to join the Breakthrough Group.*

*Breakthrough is a slow and steady process. Things didn't change over night and there were many ups and downs. The important part is to stick to it and not give up because eventually there will a moment, or many moments, during the breakthrough where you will feel the change inside you and you will know that now you have the confidence to take the next step. In my case this was in my 5th session when I spoke to the group for the first time - with me actually looking up and looking people in the eyes, instead of just looking down, as I would normally do. Although I didn't say much, I could feel a change inside me. I felt a great sense of achievement. This was the moment I realised that I could actually change myself. All it needs is a bit of time and effort. Then after my 7th session, I remember I could easily look up and talk to the group for good 3 minutes without any issues. I admit I still felt slightly nervous but I had control over my nerves. I knew that all I needed was a bit more* practice and I would be totally fine. And I was. I never had any issues performing in front of the group. In fact, it was something I loved. I also found out how good I was at acting, which is something I had no idea of before. Again the only issue I had in the beginning was to talk in front of the group while acting, which again was something I managed to overcome with time and got completely comfortable with. For some reason, I always enjoyed playing the evil king. It allowed me to express myself in a way I have had never done before. I guess it was this new feeling that made me enjoy playing the evil character. I would always receive positive feedback for my role as the evil king, and knowing that people enjoyed watching me made me feel great.

The change and progress I made through Breakthrough was absolutely priceless. This was the first ever programme that actually managed to bring about a change in me unlike every single other therapy programme I had done.

Notice how much enjoyment Stefan experienced from playing the evil king. It was on his sixth session that he had so much fun playing the evil king and his seventh when he made a significant breakthrough. There was no accident in this. As I pointed out in Chapter 8, playing out the nasty characters and playing out potent aspects of the Shadow is the key to transitioning from wallflower to sunflower. Many clients are reluctant to do this. It makes no logical sense to play a nasty character, and yet they find when they do it, they instantly feel better - more alive, more real, more true to themselves. As result, they are then able to take this into their outside life. Stefan amazed the group with his accounts of all the things he started doing in the outside world. This is typical. Once accessed in this way, the natural confidence that is within you can never be forgotten.

I believe what we are trying to do in our lives is to become more aware of what's going on inside ourselves, so that we can truly support ourselves to become the person we've always wanted to be and **deep down you know you truly are.** Through expanding into your deepest potential, you support others to do the same and you have more to give, so everyone benefits. As Marianne Williamson said, *"Our playing small does not serve the world."*

It's not easy to achieve all this without help. Amaterasu needs the myriad of gods to bring her out of the cave, and so do you. Most people make the deepest shifts with a supportive group of people who are intent on creating a breakthrough in their lives. If you feel inspired by what you have read here, please visit my website www.makingmoves.net where you will also find many additional resources.

At the time of writing I am exploring new ways of serving you, particularly anyone who is in other parts of the world or in remote places, who are unable attend my courses. If you've signed up for the bonus material I'll be keeping you informed about this. Almost every day now I receive requests from people in other parts of the UK and the world asking me if my courses are available there and, in time, I will be training up practitioners to deliver these courses. This may take a little bit time to achieve but it's something that I very much want, so that more people can experience the benefits of the Sunflower Effect.

So keep learning and growing - and this is what I add to almost every email that I send out: "I am rooting for you all the way."

There's a quote from Nietzsche: *"you still must have chaos within yourself to give birth to a dancing star".* In other words, you don't need to be perfect. You can still have chaos, you can still be a mess, you can still have things that aren't quite fixed, in fact you need those things in yourself to truly give birth to the brilliant person and the potential that lies within you. Do it. Believe it now.

## Courses to Support You in Moving from Wallflower to Sunflower through the Sunflower Effect

### Breakthrough Group

The Breakthrough Group is the course that many people do first and is designed for people who define themselves as a wallflower or feel they have shyness on their radar in any form. Over twelve weeks, you will be supported through the processes described in this book to break out of your shell at your own pace and in your own way – no matter how inhibited or stuck you feel you are - and to develop an effortless self confidence that comes from a deep place within.

### Finding Your Voice

This course is designed for people who define themselves as a wallflower in one particular area – speaking in front of groups or what is often known as public speaking. It's designed to support you to overcome your fears in a safe environment. It's unique in that it will actually dissolve the symptoms that cause you so much stress: panic attacks, beating heart, blushing and the multiple thoughts that get in the way of your communication. It's also effective at overcoming verbal blockages and inhibitions or if you feel that you are unheard by others. Many participants do this course as a follow up to Breakthrough.

## I Don't Know What to Say

Many wallflowers often feel stumped for knowing what to say, when under pressure, or in social situations. One of the reasons why you dry up or go blank is because you go into your head and **try to** think of something to say. This course uses an adapted form of improvisation that will enable you to bypass your analytic mind and enable you to respond in the most natural way. Then you will be amazed at what begins to come out of your mouth. You too will learn skills that will stand you in good stead for the rest of your life.

## Breakthrough Plus

There's a powerful link between **confidence and self-esteem,** and this is why it often so difficult to maintain confidence, when you've had painful experiences in the past that have affected your confidence and self esteem - as we have spoken about in this book. **Breakthrough Plus** is designed for those who know they have deeper work to do. It is an intensive course that takes place over two weekends. It will enable you to transform those experiences through a unique creative process – working with the story of Amaterasu that we have been exploring in this book. It will take you on a powerful journey of self-discovery opening up the pathway to breakthrough and support you on breaking through your most intractable issues.

For more information about all these courses see www.makingmoves.net or this book's website, along with further resources mentioned in this book: www.fromwallflower tosunflower.com

Printed in Great Britain
by Amazon